MEDITATIONS

for

EVERYMAN

MEDITATIONS
for
EVERYMAN

by

JOSEPH McSORLEY
Of the Paulist Fathers

In Two Volumes

Volume Two
PENTECOST TO ADVENT

DEUS BOOKS
PAULIST PRESS
(Paulist Fathers)
New York, N. Y.

A Deus Books Edition of the Paulist Press, 1963, by special arrangement with B. Herder Book Co., St. Louis, Mo.

NIHIL OBSTAT: Joseph I. Malloy, C.S.P.,
Censor Deputatus

IMPRIMI POTEST: James F. Cunningham, C.S.P.,
Superior Generalis
April 26, 1948

NIHIL OBSTAT: G. M. Guyot, C.M.
Censor Librorum

IMPRIMATUR: ✠ Joseph E. Ritter,
Archbishop of Saint Louis
May 1, 1948.

A HELP TO IDENTIFY THE SUNDAYS AFTER PENTECOST

Year	Pentecost	Second Sunday After Pentecost	Fifth Sunday After Pentecost	Eighth Sunday After Pentecost	Eleventh Sunday After Pentecost	Fourteenth Sunday After Pentecost	Seventeenth Sunday After Pentecost	Twentieth Sunday After Pentecost	Twenty-third Sunday After Pentecost	No. of Sundays* Between 23rd & Last (24th) Sunday after Pentecost.	Last (24th) Sunday After Pentecost	Year
1961	May 21	June 4	June 25	July 16	Aug. 6	Aug. 27	Sept. 17	Oct. 8	Oct. 29	3	Nov. 26	1961
1962	June 10	June 24	July 15	Aug. 5	Aug. 26	Sept. 16	Oct. 7	Oct. 28	Nov. 18	0	Nov. 25	1962
1963	June 2	June 16	July 7	July 28	Aug. 18	Sept. 8	Sept. 29	Oct. 20	Nov. 10	1	Nov. 24	1963
1964	May 17	May 31	June 21	July 12	Aug. 2	Aug. 23	Sept. 13	Oct. 4	Oct. 25	3	Nov. 22	1964
1965	June 6	June 20	July 11	Aug. 1	Aug. 22	Sept. 12	Oct. 3	Oct. 24	Nov. 14	0	Nov. 21	1965
1966	May 29	June 12	July 3	July 24	Aug. 14	Sept. 4	Sept. 25	Oct. 16	Nov. 6	1	Nov. 20	1966
1967	May 14	May 28	June 18	July 9	July 30	Aug. 20	Sept. 10	Oct. 1	Oct. 22	4	Nov. 26	1967
1968	June 2	June 16	July 7	July 28	Aug. 18	Sept. 8	Sept. 29	Oct. 20	Nov. 10	1	Nov. 24	1968
1969	May 25	June 8	June 29	July 20	Aug. 10	Aug. 31	Sept. 21	Oct. 12	Nov. 2	2	Nov. 23	1969
1970	May 17	May 31	June 21	July 12	Aug. 2	Aug. 23	Sept. 13	Oct. 4	Oct. 25	3	Nov. 22	1970
1971	May 30	June 13	July 4	July 25	Aug. 15	Sept. 5	Sept. 26	Oct. 17	Nov. 7	1	Nov. 21	1971
1972	May 21	June 4	June 25	July 16	Aug. 6	Aug. 27	Sept. 17	Oct. 8	Oct. 29	3	Nov. 26	1972
1973	June 10	June 24	July 15	Aug. 5	Aug. 26	Sept. 16	Oct. 7	Oct. 28	Nov. 18	0	Nov. 25	1973
1974	June 2	June 16	July 7	July 28	Aug. 18	Sept. 8	Sept. 29	Oct. 20	Nov. 10	1	Nov. 24	1974
1975	May 18	June 1	June 22	July 13	Aug. 3	Aug. 24	Sept. 14	Oct. 5	Oct. 26	3	Nov. 23	1975
1976	June 6	June 20	July 11	Aug. 1	Aug. 22	Sept. 12	Oct. 3	Oct. 24	Nov. 14	0	Nov. 21	1976
1977	May 29	June 12	July 3	July 24	Aug. 14	Sept. 4	Sept. 25	Oct. 16	Nov. 6	1	Nov. 20	1977
1978	May 14	May 28	June 18	July 9	July 30	Aug. 20	Sept. 10	Oct. 1	Oct. 22	4	Nov. 26	1978
1979	June 3	June 17	July 8	July 29	Aug. 19	Sept. 9	Sept. 30	Oct. 21	Nov. 11	1	Nov. 25	1979
1980	May 25	June 8	June 29	July 20	Aug. 10	Aug. 31	Sept. 21	Oct. 12	Nov. 2	2	Nov. 23	1980

* See note on page 86

CONTENTS

INTRODUCTION

THIS second volume continues the meditations for each day of the Liturgical Year. The texts—in our own words—are taken, as a rule, from one of the Sunday Gospels and bear upon a topic suggested by them; although the attempt to find a single idea for each week has not always been successful. Only in a loose sense, therefore, can each week be said to present a definite, dominant theme. This fact, however, is relatively unimportant, as the meditations are intended mainly to stimulate the reader's own thoughts and reflections.

It is suggested that the reader should:

1. Each evening, go slowly over part of the meditation for the following day, dwelling upon considerations associated with what is read.

2. The next morning, read the first and second paragraphs, making a practical application of the ideas that have occurred, and following this with whatever affective prayers and aspirations may present themselves.

3. After an interval, read the third paragraph, concluding with specific resolutions and taking care, if practicable, to make one resolution definite and dominant.

4. End with a silent Act of Adoration.

NOTE: The Bible texts are quoted from the Confraternity of Christian Doctrine version.

PENTECOST SUNDAY

We Will Come . . . and Make Our Abode with Him
(John 14, 23)

TODAY we commemorate the first Christian Pentecost when, in fulfillment of Christ's promise, the Holy Spirit descended upon the Apostles. It is but gradually that we appreciate the profound significance of this event. For it means that God Himself has come to abide with us—not only all the day long, but during the dark night as well; and this union will be more intimate, more satisfying than human love can ever be.

When He promised the Holy Spirit, Our Lord told the disciples that here in our low, earthly life, with its clouds and crosses, its burdens and temptations, each one of us is allowed to enter into close personal union with God Himself. This is like a promise to bestow upon us at least a single ray of the light of Heaven. It is a promise that we shall in this life see darkly, faintly, as in a mirror, that which the beatific vision will make clear when at last we are face to face with our supreme Good, the Blessed Trinity, Father, Son and Holy Spirit. Christ's words gave a guarantee, and the coming of the Holy Spirit gives a foretaste, of a completely satisfying and never-to-be-interrupted union with God, which will leave no rational desire of the soul unfulfilled.

Recalling all this, I adore You with new gratitude and new fervor, my Lord and my God! Present as You are to me now, may You be even more intimately present as the days and years go on—"Closer than breathing, nearer than hands and feet." While the poet thinks of You as the Creator "Whose dwelling is the light of setting suns," and the saint speaks of You as "living in light inaccessible," I ponder the fact that You have come to abide with me, so little worthy of Your coming. Because this gift is bestowed by You, I accept it; and I will regard it as my most precious treasure so long as life shall last.

God Is Spirit (John 4, 24)

WHEN we speak of God we use human words. When we picture Him we make images derived from Matter. Yet we know perfectly well that words and images are hopelessly inadequate to represent God. It is not surprising, therefore, if our first attempts to imagine the Presence of the Holy Spirit in the soul are childlishly insufficient—however sincere, however truly inspired by affection, however firmly based on sound teaching. God cannot be in a soul as water is in a container, or as a man is in a house, or even as the Body of Christ is in the tabernacle. We shall get a more helpful, although still inexact, notion of a spirit, if we liken it not to objects, but to forces—heat, gravitation, electricity, magnetism, all of which are invisible, powerful, and not easily or crudely confined.

When we affirm that a spirit is present anywhere, we mean it is active there. The manner and the degree of presence vary with the manner and degree of activity. Thus, for example, the Creator is present in man when He gives man existence, and again when He gives him intelligence; He is present in still another way when He infuses supernatural light into the soul. The coming of the Holy Spirit means that God became active in the faithful disciple as never before. He came more completely and more perfectly, enriching man with new and greater gifts.

Thus thinking, I turn my eyes within, and I say: "Dear Lord, You have been in this place and I knew it not." But now at last I recognize and I adore You! Honor and glory be unto You, O hidden God, within my soul! Forsake me never! May You be blessed and praised by every creature! Most of all, may You always be blessed and honored and served by me!

I in Them, and Thou in Me (John 17, 23)

Most of us perceive at least dimly what the saint sees clearly: that the indwelling of the Holy Spirit brings about the realization of the boldest aspirations man has ever cherished. God, to be sure, always is, always must be, present to each of His creatures. He must be present in every part of the universe to keep it from disintegrating into nothingness. But on Pentecost the Holy Spirit penetrated more deeply into the souls of His saints, bestowing upon them a gift that, in the words of Pope Leo XIII, "had never before been given in the same degree." By this unique gift the Lover and the beloved are united as both desire. Theology ascribes this loving union to the third Person of the Blessed Trinity because His distinguishing note is "procession" from the reciprocal love of the Father and the Son.

The presence of the Holy Spirit in the soul is the one possible fulfillment of a deep longing of each human heart. It is the one possible justification for the daring phrases of poets who sing of love. On a merely human level, the ideal of the lover is unattainable and his language wildly extravagant. Nature holds out no hope to those who dream of an ecstasy that will endure. But in the soul of a saint, the desire for love, perfect and everlasting, will be realized — partially here, wholly in Heaven.

This is the blessed gift in which I share. This is the vocation to which I have been called. This is the goal which I shall surely reach if I am faithful in resisting temptation and in making the most of my opportunities. Infinitely beyond my merit, but also infinitely significant of Your goodness, dear Lord, this gift of Yourself evokes the best my soul can give in thanksgiving, in affection, in adoration. Once again I give You myself, all that I am, all that I can hope to be or to possess.

Greater Love Than This No One Has (John 15, 13)

IN THE liturgy of the Church, the feast of Pentecost has a higher rank than the Feast of Christmas. That may strike us as surprising, for we are accustomed to concentrate on the Incarnation—the great central fact of faith and worship. When we begin to consider the Indwelling of the Holy Spirit, however, we quickly perceive its sublime significance. For the coming of Christ upon earth was a means to an end; and it is to this end that the feast of Pentecost directs our attention. Behind creation, behind the Incarnation, behind the Redemption, behind the institution of the Church, is the desire of God to effect a loving union with the human soul. God is a Lover in as true a sense as anyone ever was— in a truer sense than anyone else could ever be.

Let us think of all the manifestations of love—remembrance, interest, attention, concern, sympathy. Let us think of a lover who hangs upon the words of his beloved; who cares how the time of the beloved is spent; who would give health, strength, life and the whole world for the sake of the beloved. Then let us tell ourselves that all these are characteristic of the love that God bears for the soul. This is something to be pondered long and deeply. God is a Lover who is—at least equivalently—an eager, impatient Lover, One who is hurt, disappointed, wounded by our inattention, by our neglect.

Remembering that God's love for me has been shown by His coming to dwell in my soul, I am stricken by the consciousness that until now I have been so inattentive, so unappreciative. Dear Lord, help me to make the most of this blessed gift which You have bestowed on me. Give me the grace to love You everywhere and always. Uplift me with the knowledge of Your goodness. Control my feelings; rule my mind; govern my body; make my will Yours. Take complete posession of me and make my soul Your own!

You Are My Friends if You Do the Things I Command You (John 15, 14)

FRIENDSHIP is tested by the ability to work together—or even to travel together—in perfect harmony. Two persons apparently sympathetic with each other, and accustomed to think along the same lines for years, may seem ideally fitted for a partnership. Yet when they undertake a common project, they develop diversity of opinions and a clash of wills. Superficial affection turns to disagreement, dislike, perhaps hate. The phenomenon is not rare.

Something similar occurs in the spiritual life. At first we conform readily to rules laid down by lawful authority; we gladly renounce posessions, preferences, ambitions, in order to carry out God's Will. But as the years pass, self asserts its claim. We refuse—or consent only grudgingly—to render obedience when circumstances or persons irritate us. Consciously or unconsciously, frankly or secretly, we set about doing things our own way. It is of primary importance for us to understand that in the loving relationship established by the Indwelling Holy Spirit, each one of us must ever and always follow gladly the least suggestion of the divine Friend within. He has come into our souls, not to receive verbal homage, the lip service of prayers, but chiefly to enlighten the mind and to direct the will. For this purpose He bestows upon us gifts which school us in habits of prompt obedience, and enable us to achieve deeds quite above our power to do alone—fine and lovely deeds, holy and heroic deeds. During the long history of Christian sanctity, our Lady's *"Fiat,"* St. Paul's *"Quid vis?"* and Isaia's *"Mitte me,"* reverberate like echoes of dominant notes, sounded in the human soul by the Spirit of God over and over and over again.

How foolish I am, dear Lord, not to have conformed my conduct to this pattern of a perfect life! What a parody my prayers have been! Now, with new understanding, I reconsecrate my time, my strength, my life. Like our Lady, I will say "So be it." Like St. Paul, I will say, "What wilt thou?" Like Isaia, I will say "Send me!"

The Light Has Come into the World (John 3, 19)

WELL instructed Catholics, as a rule, realize the tremendous part played by the human will in collaborating with God's grace. Comparatively few appreciate the part played by the intelligence. Yet the limitations of the mind circumscribe the activities of the will. What I do depends upon what I know. If you could see precisely what I am thinking about, you could foresee how I am going to behave. There is in the will nothing which was not first in the intellect.

Once we have come to a proper notion of the mind's importance, we are on the way to a better appreciation of the gifts of knowledge and understanding which clarify and perfect our spiritual vision. As intuition supplements, and even to some extent replaces, sense experience and reasoning, these gifts intensify the light of faith. They bestow a familiarity with truth which seems almost experimental. The heavenly light, when focused upon created nature, picks out spiritual values. Directed toward revealed truth, it shows hitherto unseen implications. Then we perceive a providential purpose in events; then we correctly appraise whatever bears upon the salvation of ourselves or of others.

Chief among the shortcomings and disloyalties against which I have to guard, is sluggishness in following the light. Were I to cherish the knowledge and understanding that have been given me, they would influence decisively my habit of mind and thereby decide my course of conduct. Let me not forget the greatness of these gifts! Often things are not what they seem; but if I follow the leading of the Holy Spirit, I will see things as they really are. Lead me then, dear Lord, by means of Your kindly light. I will follow!

I Myself Will Give You . . . Wisdom (Luke 21, 15)

SPIRITUAL masters teach that wisdom is the most perfect of the gifts bestowed upon us by the Holy Spirit. Like charity, it is comprehensive. As charity implies all the other virtues, so wisdom implies all the other gifts affecting intellect and will. Like charity, too, it may be compared to the rays of the sun, bringing warmth by which to live, light by which to see. Significantly, St. John, in contrast with the other Evangelists, does not use the word "wisdom"—possibly because the word "charity" is an adequate substitute for it.

The saints who most impressively blend intellecual and mystical excellence—for example, St. John, St. Paul, St. Thomas Aquinas—illustrate the fact that anyone who embodies charity also possesses wisdom. This fact reminds us that the source of wisdom, also the best means for developing wisdom, is love. As egotism is effective in dimming, so charity is effective in sharpening, our spiritual vision. Those who love, see far and see true. They are "wise."

With the gift of wisdom, comes new ability to savor, to taste. One result of spiritual growth is to render repulsive all that is distorted, coarse, unholy. Let me learn to set my course and shape my conduct, not by the standards of the world, but by the words of Our Lord, the behavior of the saints, the tradition of the Church. May I learn to choose as a frequent subject of thought and conversation, the deeds and the sayings of souls who have shown heroic strength on the battleground of the spirit—those masterpieces of Christian wisdom and courage. I may in consequence miss rewards that worldlings give and receive; but I shall lose nothing that is worth the having, nothing that could be kept forever. And I shall be content.

In the Name of the Father, and of the Son, and of the Holy Spirit (Matt. 28, 19)

IN various places the New Testament speaks of three divine Persons—sometimes of the heavenly Father, again of the Son, again of the Holy Spirit. Were it not for the clear teaching of the Church, this diversity of names might well confuse our notion of the Deity. But, hammered out on the anvil of theological controversy during long centuries, her formulation of the dogma of the Blessed Trinity, enables us to think and speak of God without danger of going astray. She represents to us the idea of three Persons in one nature—all three co-equal, infinite, divine. Not a contradiction, yet still a mystery, this doctrine, far outside all human experience, presupposes revelation as its only possible source.

The distinction of Persons in God has to do with what theology calls His "Inner Life," not with His "External Acts." True, by a process called "appropriation," we do attribute to one of the three divine Persons some particular activity which harmonizes with His characteristics. But, in reality, when we creatures deal with God, it is always with God, One and Undivided. No one of the three Persons is ever separated, or separable, from the other two. In whatever fashion we may represent things in our imagination or in our speech, it is to the Holy and Undivided Trinity that we owe our creation, our redemption, our sanctification.

O beata Trinitas! In my contemplation of You, I learn that Love is eternal, infinite, divine. That You are Love, was true even before the creation of the world. Meditating on Your dealing with us, I learn that to You we owe every good and perfect gift—the human nature of Our Lord, His Immaculate Mother Mary, the Church, the Sacraments, and the holiness of all the saints. Turning to You in grateful recognition, I adore You, O Blessed Trinity, source of all blessings that ever have come or ever can come to me! You are the founder and origin of every good deed that has ever been done since the beginning of time, or ever shall be done until time ends!

I Will Give Thee the Keys of the Kingdom of Heaven
(Matt. 16, 19)

W E MISINTERPRET Christ's teaching and lose the very essence of His Gospel, if we look on religion as nothing more than a private relationship of the soul with God. To misunderstand Christianity thus, is to overlook some implications inherent in the very fact of the Incarnation. That the soul is to be saved by means of the body is fundamental in the New Testament. The same Jesus who bade His disciples worship His Father in spirit and in truth also told them to be baptized with water. He bade them re-enact the Last Supper in common. He commissioned the Apostles to teach and to forgive sins in His Name. He founded the Church and He made Peter its head.

Jesus saved His disciples from danger of a common human error when He instituted an authority to define His creed, to develop and apply His principles. He guarded them against self-justification when He told them to acknowledge their sins penitently to His minister. These are institutions and forms which make His disciples strikingly different from the starry-eyed idealists who act as if the things of heaven and the things of this life were divided from each other in hermetically sealed compartments. Men who hold that religion is entirely a matter of private, secret communication with God, belittle Christianity's external element. They seem, at least equivalently, to exclude the necessity of the Incarnation.

Dear Lord, help me to keep clearly in mind that I am a member of Your Church, that I am always subject to a visible authority, that those who are over me are in this respect Your representatives. Reverence, docility, alacrity in obeying—these are the proper fruits of humility. Help me to cultivate them!

Upon This Rock I Will Build My Church (Matt. 16, 18)

OUR Lord's interest in men was not limited to His contemporaries. He brought from heaven a message for all mankind and for all time—*in saecula saeculorum*. His instructions to His Apostles—especially to St. Peter—show that He planned to convey that message by means of an organized body. Some such plan would, of course, be literally indispensable if His revelation were to be communicated in its purity to generations still unborn. No oral tradition, no written record, no individual zeal however fervent, would suffice. The one possible alternative to a visible society would be an unending series of new divine revelations to safeguard and interpret the first.

Divinely commissioned to carry on Our Lord's work, and divinely equipped with the powers necessary to succeed in that undertaking, the Church is aptly described by St. Paul as The Mystical Body of Christ. The conception is that of a living organism, well adapted to its environment, absorbing new elements of growth day after day, drawing upon the best available material for its nourishment. As leaves alter their hue season by season, as animals change in appearance from youth to age, the Church too varies in accidental details but always remains, like the leaf and the animal, essentially the same. Sacramental in character, she has an outward and visible form which the eyes of history see and the hands of science touch; and also an inner invisible life which is the divine element within.

I have good reason to reproach myself for falling far short of that fervent love for Your Mystical Body which should be the badge of every true disciple of Yours, O Lord! I have had too little appreciation of the precious gift of Faith with which You have blessed me. I remind myself now of what I owe to this living teacher of truth, this healer of souls that are ill, this loving mother of saints! As I begin to realize how dark life must be to those outside the fold, I thank You, Lord, for making me a member of Your "Body, which is the Church."

1st WEEK AFTER PENTECOST—WEDNESDAY
The Works That I Do . . . Bear Witness Concerning Me
(John 10, 25)

SELDOM now do we hear echoes of the old controversy of faith *vs.* works. Our contemporaries, as a rule, have little respect for any form of religion that stresses the value of belief in God, but belittles the duty of helping a neighbor. This attitude helps to deepen men's respect for, and to facilitate their belief in, the divine origin of Catholicism. Never on the pages of history has there been a written record of beneficient deeds so many, so widespread, so uninterrputed as those credited to the Church.

It is not too much to say that life of the Church is one worthy of a society that claims the exalted title, Mystical Body of Christ. Her unique story of unselfish service in behalf of all classes and conditions; her solicitude for the poor, the weak, the afflicted—the little ones of Christ—may well be pointed out as at least a corroborating proof of her divinity. Friends learn to know and love each other through long, intimate acquaintance with each other's thoughts and activities. Thus also do persons outside as well as within the fold, arrive at a knowledge of and a deep affection for Catholicism.

When I think of the blessings that have come from the faith that You, dear Lord, implanted in the hearts of men, I am moved on the one hand to gratitude, and on the other to shame. My shame springs from the consciousness that I have taken too little part in the activities of my zealous fellow Christians. Many persons with resources no greater than mine find it possible to give what seems to me like an extraordinary amount of time and energy and material assistance. I get alarmed when I remember the picture You painted of the Last Judgment. It is not yet too late for me to do something quickly. Your words about "the testimony of works" remind me to examine my conscience again with regard to my opportunities and to try in future to participate more generously in the corporal and spiritual works of mercy.

1st WEEK AFTER PENTECOST—THURSDAY, CORPUS CHRISTI

The Bread That I Will Give Is My Flesh (John 6, 52)

THE FEAST of Corpus Christi brings to mind the Last Supper where Our Lord, having changed the bread and wine into His own Body and Blood, said to His disciples, "Do this in commemoration of Me." Never was a more solemn obligation imposed upon men; never in human history has an obligation been more splendidly fulfilled. During long centuries, the Real Presence of Our Lord in the Blessed Sacrament has given divine meaning to an outpouring of fervor from the deepest recesses of human hearts that has never been equaled.

This Presence it is that makes the atmosphere of Catholic church and Catholic chapel distinctive. Here as nowhere else man comes consciously and reverently to make contact with God. Holy Communion is the unique test that determines the fitness of the individual soul to approach its Maker. The least sentimental of men may find his heart filled with emotion when he visits the church, assists at Holy Mass, or kneels as Our Lord is carried in procession among worshiping crowds. The child at the altar-rail, the woman with closed eyes before the tabernacle, the old man who fingers his beads, are looking at the Face that wore the radiance of Tabor, the agony of Gethsemane, the shame of Calvary. They are thinking of the feet that trod the hills of Galilee, the lips that loved to pardon the penitent sinner, the fingers ever ready to break the Bread of Life for famishing souls.

Dear Lord, as I kneel before You, I know that You are telling me to grieve for my faults, to mend my ways. You, Who said once that Your sheep would hear Your voice and follow You, You will help me to rid myself of pettiness and injustice and resentment. If I yield myself to You wholeheartedly, I know I shall become what until now I never really have been—Your true disciple!

1st WEEK AFTER PENTECOST—FRIDAY
Go Into the Whole World (Mark 16, 15)

CHRIST'S sending forth of His first missionaries re-calls the whole long story of the world-wide, endless activities by which the Christian apostolate discharges its divine commission. As Christ's messenger and agent, the Church has gone into the four quarters of the world, entering every field, little or great, seeking out every nook and corner where divine seed might be planted and a divine harvest reaped. Penetrating first the far ranging provinces of the Roman empire, then settling among the untamed barbarians, she devoted herself to the task of persuading good and bad, wise and ignorant, rich and poor, to embrace the faith of Christ. She has been teaching, exhorting, warning, consoling, threatening for nineteen centuries. She has faced every sort of danger and experienced every kind of hardship; and she will continue her mission until the day of doom.

Studying the record of the Church's apostolic activities, we are stirred first by a sense of the inestimable blessings which she has brought to men. In her household souls find peace. Vision, strength, purity, power to overcome evil, belong to those who have listened to her, Christ's own messenger. Many have been rescued from spiritual illness and imminent death.

I must be sure that I utilize my own privileges as a member of Christ's fold. Over those who waste God's gift of grace there hangs a shadow of malediction and approaching woe. For all those still outside the fold, and for the dead and decaying members cut off from the life-giving flow of the Precious Blood, I must pray. I shall pray for them and try to help them; but, please God, I shall not be numbered as one of them!

1st WEEK AFTER PENTECOST—SATURDAY
The Gates of Hell Shall Not Prevail Against It
(Matt. 16, 18)

ALONE among the various Christian bodies, the Catholic Church claims to possess the divine gift of infallibility. In the teaching and the interpreting of Christ's message to mankind, she is—as He proclaimed she would be—preserved from error. The Church then is a Supreme Court, divinely established to tell us if a doctrine does or does not accord with His message, if an action does or does not harmonize with the moral principles He established. To have exercised this office during nineteen centuries without ever having been found guilty of self-contradiction, without ever having defined as true what reason can show to be false—this is evidence of divine authenticity, impressive and persuasive.

It is easy to see the theoretical value of having a divinely established court. It is almost equally easy to see that there is no other practical way by which modern man can find out precisely what Christ actually taught. Honest persons may study the Scriptures carefully and arrive at mutually contradictory conclusions. Good men may search their consciences and yet arrive at opposite views concerning the morality of a certain line of conduct. It seems fairly obvious that there has to be an infallible court to decide questions of faith and morals, if the meaning of Christ's message and its proper application to the affairs of daily life are not to disappear from the minds of men.

Let me again voice my gratitude to You, dear Lord, for having given us the Church to solve problems of faith and conduct that cannot otherwise be solved satisfactorily. As I look about me, I see the shocking ills that afflict individuals who undertake to live without the Church's guidance. I, as a Catholic, can claim God for Father and Church for mother. May I ever be a grateful and most dutiful child of this Father and this mother!

23

2nd WEEK AFTER PENTECOST—SUNDAY
A Certain Man Gave a Great Supper (Luke 14, 16)

IN THIS allegory of the householder who invited many guests to his banquet, Our Lord pictures the infinitely generous heavenly Father and the vast multitude to whom He offers precious spiritual gifts. Like guests at a table bountifully supplied, we may receive nourishing food and then go forth sufficiently strengthened to overcome every obstacle, to fulfill every obligation.

To put things very simply, one may say that on each and every occasion, God gives us whatever help we need. Or exercising the imagination one may describe the various ways in which God aids us: through the ordinary sacramental graces there flows to each of us an inexhaustible stream of pardon, of comfort, of strength; in moments of weakness we are re-enforced by the actual company of countless saints who press us forward; under the unlovely appearances of poverty and pain, God opens our eyes to perceive rich treasures. Invited to make use of all these good things, indeed we are like favored children in a loving Father's house.

I had better remind myself often how highly privileged I am in contrast with many of my fellow mortals who are spiritually undernourished, poverty-stricken, pathetically feeble. Let me, after the fashion of a child, reach eagerly for what the Father offers. There is no need for me to hesitate because I am unworthy. There is no need for me to protest my inability. It can never be a blunder to enter any door He opens. So once again, I see that I am one of the most fortunate of mankind. Nothing in all this visible world can equal my gifts in beauty or in value. The famous and the wealthy and the powerful of this world can claim no possessions comparable to mine. For I have been invited to the Supper Table of the Lord! I am His honored, privileged guest. And I have been given the Bread of Angels to feed upon!

And They All . . . Began to Excuse Themselves
(Luke 14, 18)

THE invited guests who excused themselves were presumably telling the truth. Their lame apologies seem to reveal not only insincerity, but also thinly veiled indifference, apathy, ingratitude. They paid their friend, the householder, a very unhandsome compliment by saying—at least equivalently—that his banquet was less attractive than other affairs on which they proposed to spend their time.

We do the same—substituting for farm and oxen and wife other interests even less worthy of being preferred to God. Engrossed in trivial, selfish, possibly sinful occupations, we present a not even plausible reason for our almost total neglect of spiritual opportunities. "We have no time"; "We have nothing to wear"; "What will people say"; "We forgot all about it"; "We will do it later on." Were we to tell the full truth, we should say, "We have lost our taste for the things of God"; "We are bored with talk of piety and responsibility"; "To us a bird in the hand is worth two in the bush; and we are going to make sure of getting what the world offers us."

I know that with me it comes down to the question of accepting, or of declining, God's invitation. Let me look squarely at these two alternatives: one wise, the other insanely foolish. To be sure, by dint of strenuous effort, by persistent twisting of my mind, by producing a sort of self-hypnosis, I can make black seem white and red seem green. But in reality, black is still black and red still red. The very nature of things establishes the absurdity of declining any gift of God. What He offers me will always be better than what I can get myself. If I make excuses for declining His gift, I play the madman. Dear Lord, make very plain to me my inexcusable rashness! If I value my soul's life and health and strength, I must not make excuses for declining Your invitation; I must not even keep You waiting!

None of Those Who Were Invited Shall Taste of My Supper (Luke 14, 24)

OUR Lord does not mince matters when He utters this hard saying. He leaves the apathetic in no doubt about the tragic consequences which follow not only treachery, but even mere indifference. Not to be with Christ is to be against Him. Not to accept His invitation is to lose life's best chance of happiness—or rather life's only chance. These thoughts are disturbing to lazy, fainthearted souls.

Is it not strange that many persons, habitually considerate of their neighbor's feelings, display so little consideration toward Our Lord? Since they believe in the sincerity of His love, and in the wealth of His resources, one would think they would make a quick response to any offer of His. Those who hang back—you and I, for example—should give thought to the consequences of ignoring a king's invitation. Being subjects, we cannot be non-committal. We have a duty of loyalty; and we must respond quickly.

I bring back to mind again the servant who buried his talent. If I do not gather, I scatter. To say nothing is to insult God. If I do not act, I do evil. I see that I have much need of deeper contrition and that I must do something by way of reparation. Well for me if I take to heart this lesson before I am finally set aside as one who did not appreciate his Lord's invitation, his King's command! You have been divinely patient with me, dear Master. Others, far less unresponsive than I, seem to have suffered much more. Their punishment came quickly. Mine has been long postponed. I do not know the reason why this respite has been granted me—perhaps it came through the prayers of holy friends. But this I know, that now, today—no later—I must begin to amend my ways. It would be dreadful to think that I am among that group of unhappy souls of whom Our Lord has said, "None of those who were invited shall taste of My supper!"

He Who Eats This Bread Shall Live Forever
(John 6, 59)

IT IS easy to see some of the reasons which make bread so appropriate as the sacramental form of the Blessed Eucharist. For bread is not only the chief subsistence of the human race, the staff of life; it is also a factor in the quality of that life. In other words the kind of physical being one becomes, depends upon the kind of bread one eats. Rich, nourishing bread gives a corresponding store of energy. Accordingly as I feed upon wheat, or rye, or corn, or rice, or barley, my body will take on different biological characteristics. It seems fitting enough, then, that anyone destined to become divinely strong should be nourished by heavenly Bread. I, who am called to be like Christ, must be nourished by His Body.

One who has eaten of this heavenly Food is fitted to live an endless succession of perfect days. We find the saints, even when fragile of body, so spiritually powerful that they are capable of long endurance and of heroic deeds. Strengthened by the Bread of Angels, they have energy enough for the doing of any duty, the utilizing of any opportunity.

It will be an enlightening exercise for me to study my daily routine in the light of these considerations. If I am nourished by the Body of Him who was so gentle in thought and word and deed, so forgetful of self and considerate of others, I should acquire and manifest these qualities. If I do not acquire them, something has gone wrong somewhere; and careful examination will make clear what it is. Always I will discover that the process of "assimilation" has been interrupted by my own fault. Hence my failure to grow Christlike is due chiefly to carelessness in performing my daily duties and in using my opportunities. Since the consequences of this failure grow more and more serious as time goes by, I must act at once. Dear Lord, that I may live forever as You promised, help me to grow strong!

Make Them Come In (Luke 14, 23)

EVERY normal human being is consciously free. He possesses liberty to choose between action and inaction, between this deed and that. Nevertheless, at times, we find ourselves under the influence of forces that seem almost irresistible. Emotion, surging up like a tidal wave, sweeps us away. A bright vision dazzles us; and we grope about like suddenly blinded men. A dominant personality commands; and we obey. Both civil and moral law recognize these limitations of freedom, these circumstances that mitigate wrongdoing. A man is at times under duress; while theoretically free, he is practically compelled to act as someone else dictates.

There is joy in the thought that God, too, sometimes propels us forcibly toward our goal, makes it hard for us to avoid the doing of His Will. That same Providence which overlooks the falling of no sparrow to the ground watches vigilantly over our ups and downs as we journey through life. Never has a loving parent been more solicitous of a child's welfare than God is of ours. When conscience speaks so persistently, so loudly, so importunately, it is really He who is bidding us to do this or that. It is He who draws us strongly toward a course of conduct, virtuous yet unattractive, or moves us to profess principles, sound but not popular. In so far as compulsion is compatible with freedom, He compels us.

I am fortunate indeed, to be thus divinely influenced —especially fortunate if I form the habit of responding swiftly and assenting wholeheartedly to God's "dear persuasion." With nearsighted eyes, I peer into the future uncertainly. But to God, the boundaries of space and the end of time are an open book; and I am safe if I follow His guidance. Experience shows me that perfect freedom is attained only by yielding readily to God's compulsion. "Who wears Thy yoke alone is free!"

He Who Eats My Flesh . . . Abides in Me (John 6, 57)

SOME souls are confused by the thought of God's infinity. They find it difficult to enter into personal relationship with anyone so amazingly different from and superior to all individuals of whom they have had any immediate experience. This confusion may be disastrous. It could cause religion to degenerate into a combination of superficial emotion and ineffective desire, directed toward a vaguely apprehended distant force.

The Incarnation wonderfully meets this need of ours. It brings the Creator within reach of the creature, so that the soul can concentrate all its powers upon God. It provides the imagination with a concrete, yet at the same time a divine, Object of affection. By instituting the Eucharist, Christ brings Himself into an even more intimate contact with His individual disciple.

"He who eats My flesh . . . abides in Me." This is not really "a hard saying." To me it is medicine and balm and heavenly light. There are no barriers now, and no bounds to the display of adoring fervor with which I should greet Jesus in the Sacrament of the Altar. I think of what I would instinctively say to my best friend; and I say that to Our Lord. I think of what He would wish me to do; and I plan now to do it. I keep pouring out upon Him the precious ointment of unselfish deeds and loving words. I mingle in the crowd of saints who press about Him with adoring speech or silent worship—the first disciples on fire with apostolic zeal, the white-robed martyrs, the unnamed, uncounted hosts who now form the court of Heaven. With them I repeat the words of the Song of Songs: "I found Him whom my heart loves . . . I took hold of Him and would not let Him go."

To SINNERS the image of Jesus on the Cross should symbolize the dread consequences of sin, the effect of hateful, vicious, disloyal deeds. It is an everlasting reminder of what man has done with the power entrusted to him by a loving Father. For the moment at least, goodness, truth, and beauty have been replaced by vileness, lying, horror. Hate has triumphed over love. Now to lift sinners out of the depths of depression and paralyzing remorse, Our Lord bids us behold His heart —symbol of a love which has overcome man's fiercest hate, of a love which offers us richer gifts than those we forfeited.

One of hell's bitterest pangs is the remembrance of things lost. Saddest of all sad words are these: "It might have been." Had we but foreseen the inevitable consequences of our act, had we but realized the worth of what we were about to lose, then we would have held on with all our strength to what was given us. Now we have only grief over lost opportunities and sadness at the sadness at the destruction of things lovely and holy. These are considerations to be pondered by each soul conscious of sin.

Fortunately, I am not yet dead, not yet judged or damned. To me and to every penitent sinner, the heart of Jesus brings assurance that there is no limit to His love of sinful man. In the book not yet closed, on the page not yet turned, let me be sure to set down some good things that will be credited to my account. Our Lord, Himself, is determined to make me holy—even me. I have but to accept His offer of pardoning, vitalizing grace. Send me Your grace. Most humbly will I accept it. Save me, dear Lord, or I perish.

What Man Does Not . . . Go After That Which Is Lost?
(Luke 15, 4)

OUR Lord's view of sin is well-defined, strongly emphasized, frequently re-stated. But sometimes we
fail to distinguish between His attitude toward sin and
His attitude toward the sinner. Sin, He hates; the sinner
He loves. As the Gospel indicates, His solicitude for
publicans and sinners was so marked that the Pharisees
fastened upon it as extravagant, and made it an excuse
for murmuring against Him.

It seems clear enough that a disciple of Christ is
bound to imitate his Master in concern for those
who fall. Yet some Christians quite deliberately show
their dislike for sinners. Instead of encouraging the
weak soul, they may be responsible for a second fall by
making repentance difficult. Is it not true that many
of us never think of extending a helping hand to falter-
ing men and women well within the reach of our influence? If the return of the sinner to God interests us
little, if we are loath to facilitate his conversion, even at
some cost to ourselves, our state of mind is very different from Christ's.

May this lesson impress itself upon me. Let me
never forget, dear Lord, that, as Your disciple, I am
given the privilege of assisting in Your work to save
sinners; and that to make use of this privilege is also an
obligation. Henceforth, I will keep in mind that I myself am one of those sinners whom You came to save.
May this consciousness help to make me consistently
aware of my precious privilege and of my grave obligation. It is with a deep sense of Your goodness to me
that I now renew my resolution to be always interested
in sinners and to be very patient with them. I know in
my soul that no one of them is worse than I.

Rejoice With Me, Because I Have Found My Sheep That Was Lost (Luke 15, 6)

IT IS one of human nature's best traits to find pleasure in helping others—pleasure that grows with the gravity of the danger avoided and the value of the good that has been gained. Instinctively men love to bring to others such gifts as health and strength and peace of mind. Often, at considerable risk to themselves, men brave fire and flood to aid helpless unfortunates who have been trapped. Sometimes a man will even achieve the difficult task of assisting those who have injured or offended him.

In this respect human nature reflects, at least faintly, one of the divine attributes. Man comes nearest to resembling God, "when mercy tempers justice." No characteristic of our heavenly Father is more marked than His long-suffering. If we consider the persistence with which, since the beginning of human history, His gracious invitations have been ignored or rejected, we almost begin to wonder that He has allowed the human race to survive. In dealing with us, His patience has been literally inexhaustible. The one unmistakable and comforting conclusion to be drawn from all this is that, no matter how far I have strayed away from the path of duty, no matter how obstinately I have persisted in wrongdoing, nevertheless, at this moment, I can, if I will, bring joy to the heart of Our Lord.

As I look back through life and count God's successive attempts to win me to the doing of His Will, as I begin to fear that my consistent resistance has made Him cease to care for me, I get encouragement from the text that reveals His joy over the sinner who after long delay is truly penitent. It is as if, at last, "the Hound of Heaven" has caught up with me. Now let me give God joy, by surrendering to Him unconditionally. May He help me to do what hitherto I have not done. Henceforward may His Will be my will; His pleasure, my pleasure.

There Shall Be Joy Before the Angels of God Over One Sinner Who Repents (Luke 15, 10)

IT TAKES time to appreciate all that is implied in a sinner's conversion. We know that sin is horrible; we are accustomed to look on goodness as beautiful. But we are not quite prepared for the statement that repentance is a thing glorious enough to stir even heaven to joy. Our Lord's statement should set us thinking.

Slowly we begin to see that the co-operation of human will and divine grace in a conversion implies a sort of miracle. A new precious moral quality has been created which cancels out, destroys something vile and dangerous. God's plan has been advanced a little further toward realization; the Redemption has been made in this soul actually more effective. Death has been conquered by life; evil has been turned into good. All this shows conversion to be something interior, spiritual—not a mere gesture of submission, not a momentary and superficial promise. It comes home to me with new force now, that, when Christ bids me repent of sin, He wishes me to destroy the hidden roots of selfishness in the very depths of my soul.

I cannot be merely commonplace and casual in the confession of my faults. To turn away from sin and then back to it again would seem to imply that I have not sincerely turned away at all. There must be something more than words and tears in my sorrow, if I am to give glory to God and joy to the angels. Some sting, some hurt must touch my soul, if it is really to experience a revolution. At whatever cost to myself, I must undergo a transformation. Let me make sure that I take this lesson home.

He . . . Said, I Will Not; But Afterwards He . . . Went
(Matt. 21, 29)

THEY say the man who hesitates is lost. But that saying does not always hold good. Manifestly, it does not hold good in the case of a soul for whose repentance God waits long and patiently, overlooking repeated delays and refusals. But at least it is true that his soul has run great risks. Only through the intervention of God's measureless mercy has disaster been prevented, only because He is infinitely kind and gracious does He consent to enter when the door is finally opened.

To say that we habitual sinners do not deserve this mercy is to say too little. God's patience with us seems quite beyond reason—as indeed it is. No merely human virtue could extend so far, could last so long. The elder brother in the parable, who grew indignant at the father's tenderness for the prodigal son, pointed out true facts and strong arguments to justify his resentment. But God's ways are not our ways. Facts and arguments do not reveal the hidden secrets and the inexhaustible depths of His love. Well for us that this is so.

Today, then, I may dwell upon the comforting assurance that, although so consistently weak, I have not yet been shut out from the kingdom. Tomorrow, indeed, it may be too late. But it is not too late today—an hour from now, possibly, but not at the present moment. Already I have run great risk; but God's mercy is still holding the gate ajar. Whatever I have done or left undone in the past, my fate as yet has not been settled. What if once I did say, "I will not." Let me eat my words. Let me confess that I was wrong. Dear Lord, I *will* go.

The Other Answered, I Go, Sir; But He Did Not Go
(Matt. 21, 30)

Persons who have little regard for honor substitute promise for performance very often—so often indeed, that this device has given rise to many a playful picturesque phrase—for example: "He is stalling"; "We are getting the run-around." Children try this little stratagem. Politicians are supposed to be adepts at it. But surely, when dealing with Our Lord, no disciple would consciously attempt to trick his Master. To try to put God off with fair words, is to ask for trouble. You cannot fool God even for a moment. We cannot "put something over" on the all-seeing, all-knowing One who loves truth and justice infinitely well. "The Lord is not mocked."

If we laugh behind a person's back, if we mock him by saying "Yes" and acting "No," the world reasonably enough assumes that we despise that person. Is it not clear, then, that when disobedience follows closely upon our prostestations of loyalty to God, we have offered Him a grave insult? It is hardly likely that one of us would act deliberately in this fashion. Probably we are only half aware of what we are doing. But there it is. We say "Yes" and we act "No."

A careful scrutiny of my conscience raises the question, "Am I not mocking God?" The form of my prayer may be correct and irreproachable; the generosity of my promise magnificent. So far as the words go, nothing more could be demanded or given. But it is all a matter of words only; and words do not go far. My deeds caricature my speech. They seem to belittle the Person to whom my promise has been given. I see now, dear Lord, that when I speak to You humbly but then face about and do as I please, I am outraging Your goodness. I have got to beware. I run great risk of offending You irreparably if, after having said, "I go, Sir," I do not go.

These Things You Ought to Have Done (Matt. 23, 23)

IT IS A proverb that to get things done quickly, one must go to a busy man. He and he alone will find time. This is because he divides his time according to a plan; whereas the rest of us do things at haphazard, suddenly starting and then suddenly stopping, beginning much but completing little, finding no leisure to foresee what is about to happen. We make ourselves think that we lack time when the real defect is lack of system.

Strangely enough we sometimes act thus carelessly in spiritual affairs. Lesser things get done, while God's interests are neglected. The saint endorses the rule of the practical man, "Do first things first." Except the saints, hardly anyone is consistently punctual and precise in comforming to rules—even rules which are of considerable importance. The saying "Order is heaven's first law," enshrines a fundamental truth; for order reflects the Mind of God. When everything is in order, all is well. Disorder means dirt, disease, sin.

Let me never say with regard to my spiritual duties, "I have no time." One who uses this phrase usually means he has time only for other more interesting things. Dear Lord, help me to set my life in order, to establish a right standard of values and a corresponding habit of conduct. Make plain to me the duties I have been postponing, so that I shall give priority to the things that deserve priority. There are virtues that by now should be well established; faults which should long ago have been eradicated; perhaps reparations which should have been made; perhaps resolutions that should at this instant be definite and decisive. Among these resolutions should possibly be included a long deferred deed of charity, a good confession, a specially strict retreat.

Thou Shall Not Tempt the Lord Thy God (Matt. 4, 7)

"TEMPTING God" is an enlightening phrase. It brings out clearly the danger attaching to certain deeds and habits which ordinarily get little thought. It reminds us that some men defer repentance as if they were sure of God's ultimate pardon; and meanwhile they continue to commit the same sin. This behavior is surely not trust in God; in reality it is an additional sin—wicked, because based on no solid grounds, no proper motives. It is a mockery of the virtue of Hope, being sinful by reason of defect. It comes as a result of spiritual blindness and excessive self-indulgence.

Too often, outsiders are alienated from the Church by the sight of a believer who repeatedly presents himself for pardon in confession, yet still continues in sin. Such a one's religion seems to be mere superstition. His conduct is scandalous. His abuse of God's mercy is a sort of blasphemy. Yet you and I may be in no position to cast stones at him. Even if our sins are less gross and shocking than his, our sorrow may be no more sincere.

Dear Lord, help me to realize that I dare not run the awful risk of making You wait. I must no longer presume to postpone the doing of duty just because You are amazingly gracious, incredibly patient. I know that sometimes the unused opportunity is suddenly withdrawn. Keep me from forgetting that even in trivial matters I shall become demoralized if I repeat promises without fulfilling them, if I affirm intentions which are only half honest. Let me not tempt You, my Lord and my God.

4th WEEK AFTER PENTECOST—SUNDAY
Lower Your Nets (Luke 5, 4)

Most of us get discouraged from time to time—often for reasons such as Simon Peter gave. We have labored all the night long; we have done our best. But our toil has been in vain; we have taken nothing. So we say, or we are tempted to say, "There is no use going on; I don't get anywhere. It would be more sensible, and it certainly would be pleasanter, to stop trying." To one thus weary after long, unavailing effort, Our Lord's words come as an inspiration. They move us to try again, to make St. Peter's reply our own. When the Lord says, "Keep going!" we must answer, "I will."

Let us try again then—not seven times, but seventy times seven. Eventually we shall accomplish the hitherto impossible task. We shall soften the heart of that implacable enemy; we shall conquer these restless passions, these deep-seated habits, this unruly tongue. Who dares predict that because we failed yesterday we shall fail today? "Lower the nets!"

I lower them; and immediately new, consoling reflections come. I see that God has been testing my trust, trying my perseverance. I ask myself, "Shall I gain anything by quitting? Shall I be happier if I stop trying?" The answer is "No." Although I have failed ninety-nine times, my hundredth effort may succeed; and although in a moment of depression, it is hard for me to remain calm and reasonable, down in the depths of my soul, I know that time is an indispensable element in the maturing of plans, as in the maturing of life. Even if I do not find what I seek, I may discover something far better. So be it, then, I will try again; and, please God, I shall die trying!

THE disciples could realize only dimly the import of Our Lord's promise to them; later centuries were to see its splendid fulfillment. But the words of the text recalling Our Lord's unfailing interest in the saving of souls, remind us that His life was one long series of episodes in this divine adventure; that He used His power to carry the Gospel of the kingdom of God to the ends of the earth; that every true disciple of His is necessarily a hunter of souls, a fisher of men; that apostolic zeal carries us to the point of self-forgetfulness.

Each Christian, then, must be profoundly interested in the spiritual welfare of the neighbor; must regard the giving of scandal as a heinous crime; must be ready to make great sacrifices to win unbelievers to faith and sinners to repentance. Love cannot be merely passive. Its normal outlet is zeal. Even the recluse in his hermitage, even the contemplative nun in her cell, must be profoundly concerned about, and—at least interiorly—busy with, the salvation of imperiled souls. For this is Our Lord's true work, the motive of His coming into the world.

Saints who reflect Christ's qualities never save time, or money, or health, or life, except to spend it upon other souls—a pointed reproach to those of us who expend our resources so wastefully, so selfishly. If I sit comfortably and watch while others labor, if I stay at home while so many are trooping into poverty-stricken, disease-haunted mission fields, then I must have blinded myself to the lesson taught by Our Lord in the parable of the buried talents. Is it possible to divorce the love of God from apostolic zeal? Is it lawful for me to absorb, but never communicate, knowledge? Or have I at this moment a great debt still unpaid—which I must set about settling in some fashion before I die?

4th WEEK AFTER PENTECOST—TUESDAY

The Fields Are Already White For Harvest (John 4, 35)

ONE who looks around this world of ours may easily find excuses for discouragement; there are countless facts that tend to depress us. But then, on the other hand, there is much that inspires, much that consoles, much that serves as a challenge to courage and a stimulus to zeal. It is unfortunate that we are usually more sensitive to evil than to good. We talk and think and worry about what is unpleasant, or dangerous, or terrifying. It is well from time to time to lift up our eyes to the hills, to fix our gaze on far horizons. The text above seems like a summons to do precisely this.

Each one of us can find an opportunity to labor at the gathering of the harvest, to aid Our Lord in the noblest work ever undertaken—the saving of souls. Despite all the suffering and all the evil that lie like a heavy burden upon our consciousness, we are bound to be uplifted by the prospect of increasing the precious result that actually comes from the Redemption.

We read in the history of St. Paul that, in a vision, a certain Macedonian begged him, "Come over into Macedonia and help us." Promptly St. Paul set sail. I like to think that in those circumstances, I would have done the same. But am I not in close contact with situations unmistakably similar to that which St. Paul faced? Am I not appealed to and waited for by many who might embrace the faith, if it were properly set before them? Let me not be apathetic, unresponsive. Let me spend less time and energy in selfish pursuits and more in those fields of which Christ spoke, where the harvest is so great, and the laborers are so few!

4th WEEK AFTER PENTECOST—WEDNESDAY
Go Therefore To the Crossroads (Matt. 22, 9)

THESE words may be regarded as an intimation of the catholicity of Christ's teaching. The truths He taught were intended for no privileged class, or caste, or rank. His mission recognized no bounds of jurisdiction, no limits of space or time. To be a disciple of Christ implies the excluding of every sort of prejudice, pettiness, narrowness. To one and all we are under obligation, like St. Paul.

Not every professed Christian sets his course by this chart. Not always do we measure up to the breadth and depth and height of Christ's ideal in which we are one —Jew and Greek and Barbarian, bond and free. Some of us set parochial, provincial, national, racial bounds to our sympathies. We are good to kinsfolk, old schoolmates, members of our political party; but we show antipathy for others. Yet in the measure that our sense of fellowship is narrowed by ties of blood, or convention, or personal profit, we are wanting in catholicity. This means that we distort and nullify Christ's teaching. The pagan's *"Nil humani"* proclaimed his sense of community with all mankind. But he had less reason than we to consider the whole world his country, every man his fellow citizen.

It is plain, dear Lord, that my friendship and zeal must correspond to Yours. This means that, like You, I must unselfishly befriend everyone, admitting no limits established by class, or race, or color, or wealth, or virtue, or sympathy. Just as surely as God is my Father, every man must be my brother!

It Is Impossible That Scandals Should Not Come
(Luke 17, 1)

OUR Lord established the Church to carry on until the end of time the mission confided to Him by His heavenly Father. He Himself planned the organization of the Church; He Himself bestowed upon her a divine commission; He Himself promised to protect her from error in the teaching of the truth that He had come to reveal. She began her career, fresh from the hands of the Divine Architect, pure of stain or defect, radiant with a holiness that bespoke the divine origin of the life within her.

The disciple who believes all this is dismayed when, for the first time, he comes upon facts which seem inconsistent with the Church's divine origin. In certain epochs of history, faith itself has been almost staggered at the unholiness of some who call themselves Catholic; at the corruption of some who, according to Catholic belief, held the keys of the kingdom of Heaven. The explanation of these unfortunate conditions, however, is not hard to discover. It lies in the fact that God has made the human will free. The Church, like her Master, has gone through her betrayal and her passion. And one outcome of her agony, as of His, has been external disfigurement. The truth of Catholicism is obscured, its loveliness defaced, its holiness marred by the sinful conduct of unworthy children.

But all this reminds me of a heavy responsibility that weighs upon my conscience. I, who bear the name of Christ, must recall with shame the occasions when I failed to reflect the light that shone into my soul, occasions when I failed to draw sinners and unbelievers toward Our Lord. Most of all, I recall with anxiety that verges on remorse, my exercising of evil influence upon souls for whom Christ died. These are the bitter reflections that haunt the soul of every traitor. They cause me to cry out like St. Philip Neri, "Lord, keep Thy hand on Philip this day, or Philip will betray Thee!"

You Are My Disciples, If You Have Love for One Another (John 13, 35)

THIS badge of discipline may seem easy to acquire. Actually it is very difficult. Love is the hardest, highest, most heroic, most holy activity of the soul, quite beyond the best ability of our human nature; made possible only by God's grace. We can share love which is the life of God, only in the measure that we renounce self. And in order to give self, we must first possess it. As the old proverb says, "No one gives what he does not have."

Here we begin to see something of the close relationship of patience and love. When dealing with persons very dear to us, we behave patiently even in difficult situations; we find excuses for shortcomings; we tolerate faults; we are content to serve. On the other hand, with persons we dislike, we are often impatient, simply because we have not learned to love them. From lack of self-possession, then, comes lack of patience; and lack of patience shows lack of love.

How am I to gain that self-possession which is the prerequisite of love? Obviously by achieving freedom from the bonds of selfish habits. A brief and even superficial, examination of my conduct will reveal that the usual cause of impatience and irritation is an inordinate love of self, a reluctance to surrender my own views, or change my ordinary habits—habits which keep me from exercising my God-given freedom. Let me remember that only the free can love, and that only self-denial will purchase freedom. Lord, help me to learn this lesson!

No Man Can Serve Two Masters (Matt. 6, 24)

IT IS hard to believe that the saints were really much like us, with the same human instincts, the same desires, the same defects. We are tempted to assume that the path of duty was plainer to them than to us, that grace made them easily victorious over the enemies we fail to overcome. We would like to think that at some future time we shall have fuller light and greater strength than at present; and we are tempted to await that day in order to attempt our best performance. Like pupils who hope some day to come upon a great hidden book from which their teacher draws his knowledge, we look around to find some hitherto unknown way to reach the kingdom of Heaven.

But there is no such big hidden book. The fault is in ourselves, "not in our stars." It is this will of mine which is to blame—this will so reluctant to bear painful things, so slow to attempt difficult tasks. *"Per aspera ad astra."* Hard tasks at hand must be undertaken at once —this is the "open secret" of the saints. This is the only lesson we have to learn.

Now is the acceptable time. Let me not wait for a moment when conditions will be more favorable. "Do now what thou wouldst then do," says *The Imitation*. If I use the light I have, it will go on ever increasing. If I do the best I can, God will be content. But I must choose now whether to remain the slave of comfort or the servant of duty, whether to follow the crowd in the search for wealth or follow my Master on the path where the poor and the chaste and the docile seek to reproduce His spirit. I cannot be on both sides. I cannot renounce and at the same time retain what the world values. Dear Master, help me to be truly Your disciple!

5th WEEK AFTER PENTECOST—SUNDAY
Unless Your Justice Exceeds That of the Scribes and Pharisees (Matt. 5, 20)

A s LONG as men remember the Gospel—that is to say, forever—they will look upon the Scribes and Pharisees as symbols of an unholy spirit which makes self supreme. These men serve as a caricature of religion, bringing out in high relief the features which Our Lord does not tolerate in His disciples. Those features form a sort of composite photograph of various traits, all of which originate in egotism. The capital sins are there —so many branches of the same trunk, so many manifestations of the one spirit.

We may liken the soul to a material object which remains cold so long as it is not pervaded by heat. It is hot and cold in inverse ratio; the less the one, the more the other. In like manner, the more egotism in the soul, the less does justice abound. How often this principle is illustrated in our conduct! We give lip service to justice, but disregard its claims when our own interests are at stake. The statue of justice is blindfolded to remind us that justice should be impersonal, objective. We, on the contrary, look sharply to see whether or not our own interests are involved; and we decide questions accordingly. Even when dealing with God, we weight the scales heavily in our own behalf.

The lesson is plain enough. I must ask myself, What am I thinking about most of the time? With what is my daily planning most concerned? Is my central interest "Self"? Or "Not-self"? The answer to that question tells whether I more closely resemble the Pharisee or the Christian saint. But, really, the moment I ask the question, I know the answer. Dear Lord, help me to look at life through Your eyes. Help me be less like what You condemn, more like what You want me to be!

Everyone Who Is Angry With His Brother Shall Be Liable to Judgment (Matt. 5, 22)

THESE words of Our Lord must not be passed over as an exaggeration. They are of a piece with all His teaching. He denounces in words of startling severity all who belittle gentleness, graciousness, amiability. He is consistent, therefore, in pronouncing sentence upon those who cherish anger, who call their neighbors fools, who refuse to be reconciled.

We know perfectly well that "in the course of justice none of us should see salvation." We need mercy; and in order to obtain mercy from God, we should make our own lives rich in mercy. If we are not merciful now, we shall regret it eternally. Let us look around. Perhaps there is some "beggar at the gate," waiting for a word or a sign from us—a word or a sign of forgiveness or comradeship, or sympathy. We should be merciful in the measure that we expect to receive mercy.

If Our Lord's stern words about anger amaze me, this is because I have been ignoring the spirit of the Sermon on the Mount, which epitomizes Christ's Gospel. I must open my eyes. If I cherish grievances and dislikes, if I judge rashly and unkindly, if I find fault day in and day out, if I habitually hurt the feelings of others, I can expect to have no part in Christ's heavenly kingdom. Let me then look over the record of my disagreements, quarrels, resentments. Have I been at fault—even partly? If so, what ought I to do about it? Make the answer plain to me, dear Lord!

Leave Thy Gift Before the Altar (Matt. 5, 24)

WHEN Christ warned His listeners against approaching the altar while cherishing resentment, He was merely renewing the emphasis He always placed upon the indissoluble connection between love of man and love of God. During the centuries that have elapsed since His proclamation of this principle, more than a few who bear His name have—more or less consciously —followed a line of conduct which implies that He did not mean what He said. It *is* possible, they affirm, for one to love God, while at the same time withholding love from some of one's neighbors—those, for example, who are, by human standards, undeserving of kindness, or those who, by their misconduct, have placed themselves outside the pale. There are some Christians who think it is absurd to love one's enemies.

The man who claims to love God while not loving his enemy is, in St. John's pointed phrase, a liar. It can't be done. The principle that Christ taught holds good always and everywhere, whether on the small scale or on the large. It applies to friends and relatives, to neighbors and acquaintances, to strangers and aliens—in a word, to everybody. The disciple who hates even a single individual cannot possibly be like the Master Who died praying for those who were putting Him to death.

In plain language then, because I am a Christian, I may not harbor a grudge, or cherish resentment, or plan a revenge. I may not refuse to anybody normal signs of good will and kind feeling. To be sure, crimes must be punished, and guilty persons brought to account by the proper authority; but not even in the prosecution of evildoers, or in the waging of war, is the Christian at liberty to hate. Surely I do not wish to incur Our Lord's wrath if I can, even at great cost to myself, escape it. Then let me pray and labor for those who injure me. May God help me to do this!

5th WEEK AFTER PENTECOST—WEDNESDAY

With What Difficulty Will They Who Have Riches Enter the Kingdom of God! (Mark 10, 23)

As a rule temptations to avarice trouble the rich more than the poor. The rich man faces particular problems—all the harder to deal with if, having been unaccustomed to wealth, he has suddenly grown affluent. The millionaire may be reluctant to use his income charitably and generously; he may be guilty of prodigal waste or wicked indulgence. As a homely proverb puts it, "The beggar on horseback will ride to hell."

Among the sins which cry to heaven for vengeance are: misusing this world's goods, oppressing the poor, defrauding laborers. These are typical offenses of the rich man. Because modern life is so complex and highly organized, they are often committed unconsciously and complacently. But a man may not escape responsibility by shutting his eyes, burying his head in the sand, ignoring the extent to which his activity or inactivity will affect his fellow men for weal or for woe.

So I must look into the use I make of my resources. I must endeavor to find out how my neighbor's welfare depends on the things I do and the things I leave undone. The development of a social conscience, like all growth, may well be a painful experience; but to refuse to grow will entail consequences much more painful. Am I ready to grow? Or am I trying to pretend that I have no share in keeping individuals and families and groups down on a low level, and even in pushing them back when they try to rise? It is quite probable that I am to some extent responsible for failing to help others by my words or by my vote. These are practical points on which I should examine my conscience. I must not hide behind a smoke screen. I must not wear blinders on my eyes. I must remind myself that if I am living as the rich live, I am not living like Our Lord.

One Thing Is Still Lacking to Thee (Luke 18, 22)

A MAN may have one radical defect that vitiates every thing he does. He may be dedicating his powers to the pursuit of a single unworthy end—pleasure, for example, or revenge, or popularity, or fame. Or his defect may be a comparatively minor shortcoming—an imperfect motive, a failure to persevere in a series of good deeds, a habit of complaining about discomforts. Recognition of a radical fault is of supreme importance if that fault holds us back from taking the step necessary at the moment for spiritual progress.

To have nearly attained success is failure. To miss it by a mere hairsbreadth, through willful weakness, is tragedy—a tragedy made not less but more gloomy by the nearness and the greatness of what might have been. A silken thread may keep a bird from flying. One mean act may shatter a nearly perfect relationship. The conscious substitution of my will for God's in a comparatively minor matter may bar me from the company of the saints. "A little more and how much it is; a little less and what miles away."

Do I hesitate to sever the last strands that bind me to persons and places I love, and to things I cherish? Am I unwilling to add the last straw that will bring the balance down? But this may be to endanger my eternal happiness. I must not trifle with God. Sometimes life is saved or sanctity achieved, by a narrow margin. Would it not be well to scrutinize my plans, ambitions, habits, opportunities, in the light of this illuminating thought? Only one thing is needful. Let me make sure that I do not lack it. Let me examine myself on patience and kindness and sincerity, on promptness and diligence, on self-denial and prayer. If I do all I can, I know You, dear Lord, will make up what is wanting.

Thou Didst Hide These Things from the Wise and Prudent (Matt. 11, 25)

SOPHISTICATED observers call a man "prudent" if he cleverly gains a strategic advantage over his neighbor, if by shrewd planning he avoids loss, discomfort, embarrassment. He is "prudent" when his projects bring in quick and handsome returns, when he buys and sells at the right moment, when everything he touches turns to gold. Not by mere luck, but by foresight, he "gets out from under." The other worldlings who fail look enviously at the "prudent" man.

St. Paul, however, reminds us that this "prudence of the prudent" is not so highly esteemed by God. The heavenly Father keeps His secrets hidden from the worldly-wise. Within their pattern of life, Christian behavior is a flat contradiction. The Prudence bestowed by the Holy Spirit does not make men sophisticated and shrewd; rather, it sharpens the contrast between them and the children of this world. The disciples of Christ seek the lowest place at the table, the meanest fare, the poorest clothes. They delight in seeing others succeed where they themselves have failed. They dedicate themselves to laborious, unrewarded work that often ends in obscure, painful death. And they do all this because they see life in true proportion; because the gift of Prudence has enabled them to do first things first.

Let me resemble those Christlike souls who are not smart or crafty. Let me not be busily engaged in calculating my chances of getting something for nothing, of driving a good bargain, of forging ahead of my neighbor. My chief concern should be to love and serve God and man. For this is the dictate of Christian prudence; and it is also the law of the kingdom of Heaven.

5th WEEK AFTER PENTECOST—SATURDAY
If Thou Believe Thou Shalt Behold the Glory of God
(John 11, 40)

IT WOULD seem as if no Christian could overlook the importance of faith. Our Lord laid stress upon it; the Apostles re-echoed His teaching frequently; and the Church, describing faith as the very root of holiness, affirms solemnly that without faith it is impossible to please God. Theoretically, then, every Christian must magnify faith. Yet we find fairly well instructed men and women from whose plans faith seems to have been excluded; they face life from the standpoint of practical reason; they weigh values in the scale of human experience. It becomes difficult at times to discover any striking contrast between cultivated pagans and these cultivated Christians who share both the principles and the conclusions of their unbelieving companions.

All this is so wrong that it is an equivalent denial of the Gospel. If, because we breathe the same atmosphere as our pagan fellow citizens we adopt their opinions and imitate their behavior; if we are no different from them in commercial transactions, political life, educational and domestic ideals, then Christ has spoken to us in vain. For He came to lift nature up to a level higher than its own. Common sense carries us just so far. Beyond that point we must follow a spiritual guide and rely upon a divine source of wisdom and strength.

In a conflict over issues that transcend space and time, issues that are infinite and eternal, we cannot hope to overcome the world by mere common sense and sweet reasonableness. We must move forward in the dark, that is to say, in the spirit of supernatural faith. We must depend upon something that cannot be seen or measured. In the words of the *Pange lingua: ad firmandum cor sincerum, sola fides sufficit.* It is faith that overcomes the world. I believe, O Lord. Help my unbelief!

I Have Compassion on the Crowd (Mark 8, 2)

How consoling, how reassuring, to know that Jesus feels pity for us! The heavenly Father is always an infinitely resourceful Friend—One who is concerned to relieve us in our need, to save us from the consequences of our haste, to counterbalance our thoughtlessness, our excessive zeal, even our wrongdoing. Other friends bear with our weaknesses; but they will not go so far as Our Lord to help us in our need—nor could they if they would.

Happy the soul that realizes the depth of God's compassion and the infinite extent of His power; for this realization implies that every temptation to despair is an unreasonable and blasphemous deceit. True, we have defects. We are often disloyal and reckless; we stray into situations out of which, humanly speaking, there can be no chance of emerging happily. But what may be impossible, humanly speaking, is easily within the power of God. And God will have compassion on us always—if we but throw ourselves on His mercy. Vividly, forcefully, Our Lord taught us this lesson of trust. He pointed to the grass and the sparrows and the lilies of the field, and bade us believe that we are of far greater value than they.

How well the saints, for all their sense of lowliness, realized that our souls are dear to God. This consciousness of worth in the eyes of the heavenly Father must hold me to the doing of His Will when I have to face human opposition or even when at times God seems apparently to forget me. "Let nothing disturb thee," St. Theresa said—to herself and also to me. Please God, nothing shall. Profoundly ashamed of having neglected and offended God, I yet am ready to throw myself upon His mercy, confident and unafraid. He will have compassion on me, I know. He will aid me graciously and generously according to my need.

How Many Loaves Have You? (Mark 8, 5)

ONE of Our Lord's touching characteristics is His concern with the small details of human life— those daily needs which men of genius often regard as too petty for their notice. In this respect, as Our Lord makes plain, He reflects the attributes of His heavenly Father, who uses the sun to shine on the just and the unjust, who cares for the sparrows, who goes searching for the lost sheep that has carelessly strayed away.

Our Lord's solicitude of course includes—most emphatically includes—all that concerns our souls. Many minor issues in our daily routine which call for intelligent attention and quick decision may seem too unimportant for His attention. We are disposed to think that we can take care of them ourselves, that we need not regard them as matters of conscience, nor bother God about them. So we just plod along as usual, day after day, in the same old rut. This, however, is a mistaken policy. Surgeons and technicians do not set minor details aside as insignificant—else there would be few successful operations, few safe voyages on the sea or in the air. Scientific progress would be very slow. Policemen and doctors and generals use notebooks; the artist is most solicitous about the perfect tuning of his piano or his violin. Scientists deal with fractions of a second, millionths of an ounce or of an inch.

Man must seek perfection through exact conformity to law. Without becoming unreasonable or scrupulous, I should therefore, take note of small imperfections and tendencies; I should include these in my calculations; I should return again and again to the hitherto unsuccessful experiments which promise to aid spiritual progress. The tone of my voice, the speed of my words, the look on my face, even my silence and my inactivity—these may have considerable importance. You, dear Lord, did not neglect little things; neither should I.

My Father Gives You the True Bread from Heaven
(John 6, 32)

THE miracle by which Our Lord satisfied the hunger of the multitude is at once a symbol and a proof. It is a symbol of the happiness that comes to the faithful disciple in eternity; it is a proof of Our Lord's power to bring about this happy result. The disciple has but to follow the instruction given by Our Lord through His representative. In a word, the feeding of the crowd in the desert helps us to understand that no other approach to perfect and unending joy is comparable to the path marked out for us by obedience. Followed with whole-hearted eagerness, this path will lead on earth to joy that no man can take away, and eventually to Heaven.

Only God can satisfy. One may try many substitutes but in the end, there comes always the same dissatisfaction. *Inquietum est cor nostrum.* Our souls are restless. Unless they find rest in God they can never attain anything but the wretchedness of failure and final despair. Of no man or woman in the whole long history of our race can it be said that the possession of natural goods or a career of uninterrupted "success" brought final contentment. Least of all can one be satisfied with natural goods if these are purchased at the cost of losing God.

Let me then re-chart my course. Let me set sail for the one haven where rest is to be found. Only the pearl of great price can give me true joy; and please God, it will. When I am hurt by human neglect, or discouraged by failure, or depressed by loneliness or pain, I will imagine what misery such a condition would bring if it were endless; and with God's help, I will take the means necessary to keep me from ever becoming a soul eternally unsatisfied.

If I Send Them Away . . . They Will Faint on the Way
(Mark 8, 3)

OUR Blessed Saviour's pity for human suffering is one of His most striking characteristics. In the parables He told, in the precepts He laid down, in the deeds He did, we find deep sympathy and tender compassion manifested over and over again. No matter who is suffering, no matter of what sort the affliction may be, here is Jesus, with kindly look and loving word and healing touch, bringing balm of heaven to every tired body and every tortured heart.

In this as in all other things, He is the model set before us for our imitation. In this, as in all other qualities, He displays the perfect type of soul. He reveals to us a spirit which, if universal, would counteract and overcome the ills and pains of all humanity. The point for me to note particularly is that Christ recognizes in every sufferer, one who has a claim upon His attention and His aid. The great curse of an afflicted person is to have no friend to give him a hearing. Everybody admits that poverty should be relieved, suffering allayed, wrongs righted; but not everybody feels that he himself should see to the relief of this poor man, or the righting of this wronged woman. Nothing shines out more impressively, more splendidly in the character of Christ than His tireless readiness to aid, His sense of being bound to help all in need of help.

It is plain then, that I cannot discharge my obligations as man and as Christian unless I look upon my suffering and needy brethren in the spirit of Christ who pityingly contemplates the hungry crowd and determines to assist them. In those who suffer and are in want I must recognize a claim upon my compassion. Whether poor, or ignorant, or irreligious, or wicked, or physically diseased, they are my creditors; I am in debt to them. If I do nothing to help them, they may bear witness against me at the last day and I shall be condemned. Let me awake this day to a sense of my obligations!

How Is It That You Do Not Yet Understand?
(Mark 8, 21)

TIME after time, by word as by example, Our Lord instructs us that we must, in our daily actions, illustrate the strength of the faith within us. We must bear fruit, or we shall be cut down like the barren fig tree. We must trade with our talent, or we shall be condemned as negligent. If we turn away from him who asks of us, if we refuse to share our abundance with the poor, we shall hardly attain the kingdom of Heaven. Thus does Our Lord, ever and again, insist upon the necessity of good works.

We may at first fail to see why good works are so indispensable; but this is only because we forget that a man's deeds offer a sure indication of the state of his soul. In His earthly life, Our Lord carried light and comfort to all; and we shall do likewise if our hearts abound with His goodness and His truth. It is not easy by introspection to decide how firm is our faith, how true our love; but it is easy to apply a decisive external test. St. John asks, "He who . . . sees his brother in need and closes his heart to him, how does the love of God abide in him?" When we look upon the great harvest fields awaiting laborers, and, on the other hand, count the immense number of Our Lord's professed disciples, we know that something must be wrong somewhere.

This is a point on which I may well examine myself. Have I taken Our Lord's repeated admonitions to heart? Am I bearing fruit? Do I display more zeal than those who have not had the gift of faith bestowed upon them? I know I am never too poor to give an alms, I know there is never a day that I cannot do something to spread the truth. Let me weigh this well.

**Blessed Are You When Men . . . Speaking Falsely, Say
All Manner of Evil Against You, for My Sake
(Matt. 5, 11)**

OUR Lord warns us that in the building up of kingdom of God, His disciples will meet with criticism. There are men and women—even among those who call themselves Christians—ready to find fault, with or without reason. When a neighbor succeeds, they explain away his success. If he stumbles, they quickly spread news of his misfortune. They recall forgotten faults; they suggest possible weaknesses. In one way or another, they turn public opinion against the victim of their criticism. Sometimes the world seems filled with these critics.

It happens then, that a man, bent upon doing what good he can, may be blocked and crippled by unkind comment and cruel censure. As a result his interest may flag, his enthusiasm cool. He may feel like dropping the activities in which he is engaged. Such is the deadening power of the bad heart, the evil eye, the bitter tongue. It is worth noting moreover, that persons who never try to do useful things themselves, often try to keep others from accomplishing anything.

There is more than one lesson for me in all this. First, I must so live that whatever evil is spoken against me will always be untrue. Again, when I encounter criticism in the doing of my duty, I must take it in my stride, as something not wholly unexpected. Most important of all, I must be sure that I myself am never guilty of speaking evil of others—especially of those who are trying to serve their neighbors. Let me ask myself: Are men being helped or hindered by me in their attempts to do good? Do I uplift or depress them? Is it love or hate that goes out from my heart?

My Food Is to Do the Will of Him Who Sent Me
(John 4, 34)

LIFE depends on food; self-preservation is the first law of nature; no other human craving is so imperative as hunger. Our Lord compares our overmastering hunger for food to His longing to do His Father's Will. And He leads us to understand that, however insistently nature may demand nourishment for the body, the soul with even greater insistence demands the food of obedience to the Will of God.

Critics sometimes accuse a saint of paying too little attention to nature. They say, "This man does not even eat enough; he exhausts himself by working overtime; he sleeps too little." Now to be sure, the principle that all excess is wrong applies even to activities undertaken for the sake of self-discipline, or in behalf of one's neighbor. But then, at the other end of the scale from excess, there is the possibility of defect—some persons work and pray too little. They exercise too little restraint over their craving for food and sleep and fun. If we contrast these two groups, we shall find that the greater amount of harm to the larger number of people results not from excessive self-discipline, but from excessive self-indulgence.

In view of all this, I should examine my conduct in order to discover toward which of the two extremes above described I habitually tend. Probably I shall find that I run very little risk of excessive self-denial, but very great risk of self-indulgence. It would be a good thing for me to regard each day of mine as wasted unless, during its course, I have nourished my soul with the kind of food that gave strength and satisfaction to the saints. I, too, was sent into the world to serve God. Of me, too, is it true that my food is to do His Will. And I shall thrive and grow strong only if I spend myself in daily obedience to the Father's Will and in the service of my neighbor.

Beware of False Prophets (Matt. 7, 15)

A PROPHET is a teacher. We all need to be taught, to be guided. In only a very small area of life can we find our way unaided. Outside of these narrow limits we depend upon others for help, passed on to us as an inheritance or bestowed upon us by those with whom we come in contact. In all the realm of living creatures, few types are more dependent than human beings. This is so obvious in the physical order that no one ignores it; yet, in the intellectual and religious world, many are unaware of the need to be guided. They do not see the dangers of false teaching. They forget, for example, that savages have done cruel and horrible deeds apparently in good faith, because they have been badly taught.

Our Lord's words have been remembered by His disciples down through the ages. History shows how solicitous each generation has been to cling to His authentic teaching. To say, "It does not matter what a man believes," has properly been regarded as an attack on the very essence of Christianity. It is bad philosophy, too, for it seems to imply that there is no objective truth outside the mind to which the mind itself must be adjusted. It seems to imply that spiritual facts are less real than those of the physical world.

These reflections fill me with gratitude that I have been made acquainted with the Gospel of Jesus, that I am able to read and meditate on the teaching of the Prophet of prophets, greatest teacher in all human history. Let me keep clear then, of every influence that might dim my faith or cloud my conscience. Let me be a pupil worthy of the training I have received. I am thankful that the Catholic Church preserves for me the true meaning of what Our Lord said and of what He did when He was showing us the way of eternal life. Thanks be to the Father, and to the Son and to the Holy Spirit!

False Prophets, Who Come to You in Sheep's Clothing
(Matt. 7, 15)

A MONG life's sad experiences is that of disillusionment. In maturity it seems quite incredible to us that a short time ago we were so guileless, naïve, unsophisticated. Looking back on those days, we recall how easily we trusted people; how ready we were to take them at face value; how, almost unconsciously, we copied fashions and ways of speech, or adopted political views, habits of conduct, moral principles.

Using a pastoral figure easily understood by His hearers, Jesus tells us there are some presentable persons whom we cannot afford to trust. Eternal vigilance is the price of holiness as well as of liberty. St. Paul bids the Galatians distrust anyone who preaches a different gospel, even though it be an angel from Heaven. This means that we must be able to pierce through the disguises worn at times by impressive persons, by friends who profess high principles. In accepting guidance we should keep continually asking ourselves: "Is this the true teaching of Our Lord?" "Is this according to the custom of the saints?" "Is this in harmony with the mind of the Church?" If we fail to apply these tests, we may find ourselves imperceptibly, but effectually, influenced by the spirit of the world so that observers would find our conduct indistinguishable from that of the pagans among whom we live.

I must be particularly watchful of the influence to which I subject myself, for I am strangely ready to welcome teachers and guides who offer me spiritual bargains, special rates, short cuts—a painless path to the kingdom of Heaven. I know that the readiest traitor is the one who keeps thinking of the high cost of loyalty and the rich reward of treason. I know that an imposter wins his easiest victories over those who wish to be deceived. Therefore, I must tell myself again, once for all, God's interests are my interests, and I shall surely come to grief if I wander from the presence of the Good Shepherd!

Inwardly Are Ravenous Wolves (Matt. 7, 15)

WHO are they, these fierce enemies of the soul thus denounced by Jesus? They are the unscrupulous teachers, who day by day inoculate minds with error; they are writers amassing wealth from the sale of books which seduce people from faith in God and from belief in a moral law. These false prophets may be spiritual aliens coming from un-Christian or anti-Christian schools of thought; at times they are persons who share our own religious tradition, at least in part at times they are dim-sighted brethren who misinterpret or modify the changeless truth of the Gospel.

Roughly speaking, the attempts to break down the Catholic conscience fall into three groups: those that belittle tradition and authority, encouraging me to make myself the judge of what is good and true; those that urge me not to be old-fashioned, or puritanical, or a kill-joy, or a spoil sport, but to stay with the crowd, follow traffic, keep in step; and those who question the very existence of the supernatural world, ignore grace, and consider that a man's only necessary equipment is a keen intelligence and strong will.

Many have been harmed by these false prophets who find an opening for their wedge of error in the fact that the ideals of Jesus are too bright for human eyes, too heroic for human will until grace comes to the aid of nature. I dare not say that therefore I must, by habitual meditation and by careful self-examination, keep myself sensitive to Christ's influence. Now and again leaders will appear, minimizing the stern ideal of the Cross, proposing a moral code which appears to be more reasonable than Christ's, pointing out a smoother path to happiness than that which Jesus trod. Of all such I must beware. I must have my answer to them ready.

By Their Fruits You Will Know Them (Matt. 7, 16)

THESE words of Our Lord tell me how to distinguish between the true teacher and the false prophet—"By their fruits." It is a test that may be applied to Jesus and His teaching; one of the strongest arguments for His divinity is the conduct of His followers.

Think of the unending procession of men and women who have embodied His ideals in lives of heroic unselfishness. Do they not form a proof of His supernatural wisdom and goodness — even as a brilliant galaxy of stars will reflect something of the Creator's attributes? No false prophet could have inspired those thousands of saints, canonized and uncanonized, whose likeness to Jesus is clear as their likeness to God, whose kinship to one another, over vast stretches of time and space, hints at the true catholicity of their ideals—for example, Paul, Augustine, Francis, Agnes, Cecilia, Teresa, and countless others.

Bringing these things to mind, I realize my own responsibility to help in the demonstration of Christian truth by showing its influence over my conduct. But I must admit that, as a mirror of Christian holiness, I leave much to be desired. I cannot say that those who observe me will see the effects of divine grace. They can hardly deduce from my behavior that frequent confession keeps one humble; that frequent Communion makes one gracious and considerate of others; that prayer gives the soul a quality of serenity and unselfishness quite distinct from, and superior to, the best that paganism can produce. Not in my life, alas, will critical observers discover the heroic virtue which is the fruit of true faith. But at last I can recognize and admit my shortcomings in the past; and I can try to do better in the future.

A Good Tree Cannot Bear Bad Fruit (Matt. 7, 18)

IT IS not hard to find persons who behave well some of the time, who pray occasionally, who give aid to their neighbors now and again. But it is very hard to find persons who behave well all the time, who keep in communion with God continually, who discharge to the full their duties of justice and of charity toward their fellow man. In a word, it is easy enough to begin; anyone can do that much. But to persevere to the end without a blot upon one's shield, without a single missed opportunity on one's record—this seems to be no more than a vision, an aspiration.

The words of Jesus may be considered as an echo of the almost terrifying call to perfection which He issued on other occasions. "The disciple must be like his Master." "Be ye perfect as your heavenly Father is perfect." He seems to be literally a perfectionist—that is, one who will not be content with, or accept, anything short of perfection. Impossible as this aim really is to unaided nature, it is nevertheless set before us—the goal which was the desire of all the saints! It was because they set their eyes on this distant horizon, because they had the courage to attempt these apparently insurmountable steeps, that they have become an everlasting inspiration to lesser souls.

Meditating on this summons to live heroically, I find my one consolation in the belief that what God wills He is surely going to accomplish, if I lend Him the co-operation of wholehearted good will. I have only to be motivated by the single desire of carrying out my orders, following my Leader, dying if need be in the loyal attempt to fulfill His command. I must try, and try, and never stop trying!

The Bad Tree Bears Bad Fruit (Matt. 7, 17)

WHEN a man sins, he does so in expectation of a reward. He hopes to be paid in money, in honor, in power or in pleasure. But the pay he really receives is suffering. It may be slow in coming; yet it is sure to come. Perhaps it will be paid out as his just reward at the very moment when he thinks he is beginning a long term of happiness as a result of having yielded to temptation. We cannot hide from God's eye; we cannot evade the working out of His eternal law. He may move slowly; but He makes no mistakes.

By God's decree the soul that sins shall die. "The wages of sin are death." Conscience tells no lie when it bids us beware of neglecting or disobeying God's command. To be sure, the world denies this truth, although it is written on the heart of man. To be sure, passion twists our judgment. To be sure, the evil spirit dazzles us with the prospect of honor and pleasure and bids us gain these by sin. But it is all a lie—one huge conspiracy to deceive us. Let world and flesh and devil cry never so loudly, speak never so glibly, sing never so sweetly—he alone is wise who believes them not.

I must brand this on my mind indelibly—I can never by sin gain anything worth having, any more than I can defy the laws of nature. Pain will follow sin just as surely as death follows life. This is the truth that I must keep before my eyes when assailed by some temptation hard to resist. I must remember that the pleasant surface of temptation hides poison, danger, death. During uncounted centuries, sinners have taken a chance; and everyone of them has lost. I cannot doubt that if I sin, I, too, shall find that the wages of sin are death!

Not Everyone Who Says to Me, Lord, Lord (Matt. 7, 21)

IN SPIRITUAL, as in commercial, affairs the rule "accept no substitute" is a good one. In both fields, however, it is frequently disregarded. We seek a substitute for that whole-souled devotedness to God which is the very essence of religion. We give lip service by saying "Lord, Lord"; we kneel down at home or in church; we dwell upon sacred thoughts and images, and read pious books —perhaps we even speak and write about the things of the spirit fluently and persuasively. Yet all of us except the saints shrink away, in lesser or greater degree, from doing the essential thing—which is to give ourselves to God perfectly by conforming to His Will.

Our Lord makes plain that fine words and good conduct are at best only the evidence, the symptom, the consequence of being a religious man. The indispensable condition for admission to the Kingdom is an interior quality. It is not enough for us to recognize this truth intellectually. We must embody it in a daily routine of wholehearted consecration—an ideal admittedly difficult, because divine.

The old saying, "All is in the point of view," is an exaggeration; but it conveys a truth. As I change my position from one place to another, I alter my physical relation to the whole universe; and something like this takes place in the spiritual order when I assume a new attitude toward God. This change is clear in the saint who turns from sin and selfishness to holiness and love. It occurs at times in ordinary men and women who respond to some inner illumination and once for all face God wholeheartedly. Has it taken place in me? Or am I reciting formulas, repeating prayers, only half-attentive to what I say, and less than half in earnest? Here is opportunity for amendment; here is material for resolution. Let me face reality. If I am not perfectly obedient to the Will of God, I am to that extent disqualified for Heaven.

8th WEEK AFTER PENTECOST—SUNDAY

A Certain Rich Man . . . Had a Steward (Luke 16, 1)

THE idea of stewardship is central in the teaching of Jesus. Without it, indeed, no one can take a truly Christian attitude toward life. With regard not only to material possessions, but also other persons; in our disposal of time; in our employment of the faculties of mind and body; in the use of everything that comes under our influence or control in the slightest degree—in all these relations we are never absolute masters, ultimate owners, but simply stewards. Eventually each one of us will be called upon for an accounting.

Having this in mind, let us fix our attention at present on the idea of stewardship as understood by the divine Teacher. The very thought that comes to us is that Our Lord's insistence on the very idea is particularly strong because of our own instinctively strong and stubborn resistance to the lesson He wishes to teach us. Habitually, egotism divides things into two great categories of "mine" and "not mine." There is a sort of emotional block to acceptance of the principle that we are not and never can be anything more than stewards.

I find it hard to uproot the prejudice which disposes me to think of myself as free; I find it hard to rate myself at zero. Yet if I am to thrive spiritually, I must realize my own poverty, my own utter helplessness. Reflecting on this, I begin to understand better than before, the seemingly extravagant words used by the saints when describing their own shortcomings. I see that my egotism is continually enroaching upon God's rights; that it keeps me from ever attaining to an act of perfect adoration. For to adore is to acknowledge with my whole being the infinity of God and my own nothingness. Let me say now with my whole heart: Dear God, You are the Master; I am the steward. Nothing that I possess is my own. It all belongs to You. And I am glad that is Yours!

He Who Is Unjust in a Very Little Thing, Is Unjust Also in Much (Luke 16, 10)

OBVIOUSLY there is purpose in God's creation of man. When He bestowed upon us the extraordinary gift of free will, He intended us to use that will in the furthering of His purpose. It is man's destiny to create things that have moral value, good deeds that leave the universe richer than before and last forever. Unless all this is true, we find it difficult to discover the reason behind the facts which our faith bids us accept as true.

The fruits of the earth and all other good things are to be enjoyed in the fulfilling of a destiny which is divinely planned. Man is given material to work with—earth, for example, and seeds which may be planted and cultivated. He cannot make things exist, but he can make them grow. Once we realize that we are God's stewards, we see clearly that it will not be enough merely to give back what has been given us. We cannot pass our time in drowsy procrastination. We have to trade like the merchant, watch and work like the fisherman, plant, water and prune like the farmer.

The record does not show that I have been a faithful steward. My books are so badly out of balance, that, if I were to be summoned before You this day, dear Lord, I should be like one of those embezzlers or forgers, deeply entangled in dishonest transactions and unable to extricate themselves. Keep my eyes open so that, from now on, I shall check my conduct more carefully, examine my conscience more thoroughly. Help me to become a faithful servant in the use of all my gifts—bodily senses, imagination, intelligence, will, and most especially, in the use of those rich graces with which You so generously endow me.

Thou Canst Be Steward No Longer (Luke 16, 2)

ST. Francis in his celebrated "Song to the Sun" glorifies God's goodness to man. Other lesser persons, too, find joy in enumerating God's gifts, sometimes setting them in a sort of hierarchy, deciding which could be least spared, which provoke deepest sentiments of gratitude. It would be possible and also profitable to attempt to discover which of God's gifts we have employed to best advantage, and which gifts we have most often or most flagrantly abused—sight, or speech, or hearing, or taste, or touch, or the power to move, or the power to think.

Among God's blessings—as anyone will quickly perceive—His gift to us of time possesses a definite excellence, because so closely associated with the gift of life. The two are, in fact, inseparable; for they come and they go together. While there is life, there is time. When life ends, time ends. If we try to get an image of eternity, we can say only that it is like time without end. It is not extravagant then, to think of time as the greatest of God's gifts in the natural order, and to conclude from this that time is the gift of which we should take best care.

Minutes are far more precious than dollars; for I can do incomparably more with my time than a millionaire could do with his wealth. Were he to throw all his material possessions into the crater of a live volcano, he would not be wasing as much treasure as I waste when I spend precious time foolishly in idle thoughts, in silly talk, in selfish deeds. Let me come to the point of all this by asking myself a specific question: What did I do with those tens of thousands of seconds that God entrusted to me yesterday? And what do I propose to do with my time today?

He Who Has Persevered to the End, Will Be Saved
(Matt. 10, 22)

IT is easy enough to promise and almost equally easy to begin. But it is hard to persevere. Persistence in the face of difficulties usually attracts admiration, for the reason that it is rare. The runner who staggers but will not quit; the swimmer who drags himself to shore after long hours in water cold enough to numb the muscles; the student who fails again and again, but eventually succeeds—these win general praise. Perseverance ranks as a valuable human characteristic; and the spiritual counterpart of this natural persistence rates high in the kingdom of Heaven. It is he that perseveres unto the end who is saved.

To devote oneself to a task that seems never ending, and to keep plodding along at it from a sense of duty; to accept at face value the divine command to hold on even though there be no visible chance of success—this is to show a gallant spirit in our dealing with God. It is this spirit which moves us to continue doing what for God's sake we have begun, and to keep going to the very limit of our ability, come weal come woe, come fair or stormy weather.

I shall make up my mind then to persist in the attempt to overcome my faults. If at first I don't succeed, I shall try, try again. I know that the disciple who struggles against long continued or oft repeated temptation, will surely receive from Christ the strength he needs. Therefore, whenever humanly speaking, I seem to have come to "the end of my rope," I will refuse to quit; I will remember that the runner who refuses to stop at the first feeling of exhaustion gets his second wind. When my strength seems to be spent, when the task assigned seems impossible, let me join the long line of those to whom trust in Our Lord's goodness has brought the courage to persevere!

Make an Accounting of Thy Stewardship (Luke 16, 2)

ONE DAY we shall receive a summons from God. The solid earth will sink from beneath our feet; the voices of those we love will grow faint and their faces fade away. Hands and feet will grow cold and numb as life slowly ebbs. Then loud as a trumpet will sound the command: "Make an accounting of thy stewardship!" It is the all-seeing God who speaks; and He cannot be answered with an excuse or a lie.

What shall we say, we who have been so unfaithful? We were given splendid powers of body and soul. Within us was the possibility of a life lovely with virtue's unspeakable loveliness. A few years of faithful labor would bring the sure reward of joy too great for the mind of man to conceive. But now into our minds comes the memory of wasted moments, idle words, wicked acts. The thought of these things will strike us dumb with fear.

In the light of that summons which I know will surely come, let me look back now over the years of my stewardship. Let me ask myself, would I be judged worthy of reward if I were called to render my accounting at this present hour? Would I be reckoned as a faithful steward, I who have neglected good inspirations, wasted sacramental graces, turned a deaf ear to advice and to warnings, rejected countless opportunities of repentance? I grow ashamed and frightened when I note that around me are many souls who clearly deserve to be regarded as faithful stewards, although they have heavier burdens, stronger temptations, fewer helps than I. Dear Lord, may I become more like them, under the inspiration of their good example and with the aid of Your grace. May I so live that I shall not be terror-stricken when I am called to give an account of my stewardship!

The Children of This World . . . Are More Prudent Than the Children of the Light (Luke 16, 8)

WHEN Our Lord drew attention to the dishonesty of the unjust steward, He bade us note also the diligence and resourcefulness with which the children of this world pursue their chosen aim. He asks us to consider the contrast in zeal between us who profess to have our hearts set upon Heaven, and those others who quite frankly are busy with acquiring tangible material goods. Plainly the contrast is not in our favor.

Let us attempt to sum up the situation. We have received "the spirit of adoption." We are children of God, joint heirs with Christ. We declare that we have put off the works of darkness. We promise that there will be nothing in our conduct inconsistent with our dignity as "children of the light." Yet in the comings and goings of our busy days; in shops and offices and stores; in schoolrooms and houses; in our buying and selling; in teaching and toiling, we do not habitually act in wholehearted conformity with our Christian profession. It is quite otherwise with the children of this world. Having no part with Christ, they do seriously attempt to make friends with the mammon of iniquity. Having put their trust in the things of the world, they live in accord with the pattern of life they have adopted. They seem to be much wiser than we are. An observer would not mistake the children of this world for Christians; but perhaps he might mistake many Christians for children of this world.

I must, therefore, make sure that my ways are not like the ways of pagan men. There must be in my conduct not the slightest element of dishonesty or injustice. I must not take part in deals which the Christian instinct denounces as wrong—even though the children of the world may smile, and call these things only "sharp practice." Dear Lord, help me to walk honestly as in the day; to act as if I were truly led by Your holy Spirit; to be unmistakably one of the children of Light!

The Master Commended the Unjust Steward
(Luke 16, 8)

THE story of the unjust steward is a fascinating parable. It impresses upon us forcibly the truth that we can learn something from all types of people, even sinners. From the present allegory, we get a lesson in foresight—one should plan for the future which he knows is approaching. We get also a lesson in ingenuity —one should take the steps that lead to the end desired, whatever it may be. Hence Our Lord sets before us the figure of the unjust steward and recommends us to employ, in spiritual affairs, a degree of foresight and diligence comparable to this man's.

Everyone knows that only by means of methodical planning do men ordinarily succeed in business, sport, war. The men who fail are commonly unwise, weak, apathetic, by contrast with their successful neighbors. If we look carefully into the qualities which make the saint different from the average person, we shall see why it happens that the saint grows spiritually rich while the rest of us go bankrupt. He lives by rule. The task we find hardest of all is that of living by rule, planning a schedule for the week, and keeping faithful to it day by day. What plausible excuses we offer for departures from our schedule! How numerous those excuses are! How glibly we present them. And how well, in our secret souls, we know that they are false!

To plan, to plan, to plan! That is what I find so hard. Even harder is it to stick to my plan faithfully, day after day. But this is so obviously and so essentially my need, that I can surely not afford to disregard the lesson conveyed by Our Lord's commendation of the unjust steward. Let me then resolve, definitely, to spend much time in carefully planning, so that I can devote more energy; mental and physical, to the things of God. Let me budget my time with generous attention to my neighbor's needs and my own spiritual welfare. Let me be alive and alert, so that when I am confronted by duty or by temptation, I shall be well prepared!

If Thou Hadst Known . . . the Things That Are for Thy Peace (Luke 19, 42)

To BE ignorant of the future is man's common lot. The exceptional individual who possesses uncanny ability to predict the future is numbered among fortune's favorites—even if he is only a day, or an hour, ahead of the event! Crowds surround him, hang on his words, follow his footsteps, take risks on his forecast. But, as we all know, this power to foretell events is rare. Chemical elements follow a plan. An eclipse, the advent of a comet, to some extent the weather, can be foretold. But a great multitude of interlocking phenomena makes many a situation too complicated for human calculations; and when we consider the interference of human wills, then future events are literally unpredictable.

In the text, Our Lord draws attention to a foolish choice and to its fatal consequences. He contrasts the happiness that would have been secured by choosing one alternative, with the actual wretchedness which followed the choosing of the other. Had the people of Jerusalem realized what they were doing, their fate would have been very different. Our Lord notes this, not merely in order to record a sad chapter of human history, but by way of instruction and guidance. Reasonable men learn by the experience of others; the sequel of decisions unwisely made forces them to be more cautious.

I say to myself: Had I but known what was good for me, much of my conduct would have been more wisely planned. It will be good for me now to think about some of the choices I would have made had I foreseen the future. Instinctively I am accustomed to blot out the memory of past mistakes and to ignore the connection between them and my subsequent unhappiness. In future therefore, I must try hard to impress myself with a sense of the misfortunes that have come upon me through my own foolish words, deeds, and omissions. Perhaps by examining my present plans, I shall discover that this very day I am planning to do foolish things. If so, let me be wise enough to change those plans; so that I may never say sorrowfully, "Had I but known!"

9th WEEK AFTER PENTECOST—MONDAY
Thou Hast Not Known the Time of Thy Visitation
(Luke 19, 44)

SUFFERING looms large in human life. We learn much about a man's character by observing the way in which he conducts himself under the threat of pain, or in the presence of pain. There are strange theories abroad—for example: that pain is an unmitigated evil; that we should use all our resources to eliminate pain; that pain is nothing but a figment of the imagination. On the other hand, Our Lord redeemed the world by suffering; and He made the Cross the glorious symbol of His Gospel.

When we note how many persons have transformed suffering into an occasion of joy, we realize that the Christian regards hardship and discomfort as the raw material of holiness. When these things come to him, he recognizes them as a visit from God. At baptism the priest says to the neophyte, "Receive the sign of the Cross, both on the forehead and on the heart, and so conduct thyself that thou mayst be the temple of God." Inspired by this ideal, the saints find their sure path to Heaven along the royal road of the Holy Cross. Their experience has demonstrated the truth of St. Paul's words: "For those who love God, all things work together unto good."

I must recognize the beneficient qualities of suffering. I must remember that, in my own life, pain is not only a cross for me to bear, but a medium of grace if I am properly disposed. To reach Heaven I must, like the saints, follow my Master along the way of sorrow. How many times, dear Lord, You have given me an opportunity to acquire a certain degree of resemblance to You by suffering patiently the painful experiences which Your providence permits to come upon me. Help me to be thus patient in future. Then I shall not be held back from peace and joy, either by evil spirits or by evil men.

One Greater Than the Temple Is Here (Matt. 12, 6)

OUR Lord impresses His hearers with a sense of God's greatness by setting it in contrast with the most magnificent object in their world—the temple of Jerusalem, which ranked among the noblest buildings of antiquity. Today we may undertake a similar contrast by thinking of St. Peter's, the Lateran in Rome, a cathedral in Milan, Cologne, Canterbury, Paris, or the most majestic structure with which we are familiar in our own country. Using some such splendid object as a term of comparison, we see it dwindle into insignificance when contrasted with the greatness of God.

God's infinite greatness, His incomparable majesty, is one of the fundamental truths which Our Lord repeated again and again—unfortunately, without lasting effect on many of us. How weak a hold we have on this truth may be illustrated by looking at the index of a weekly magazine, or a Sunday newspaper, and noting the topics which, according to experts, chiefly attract our interest —amusements, art, books, business, cinema, comics, education, fashion, food, medicine, music, politics, radio, science, sport, stocks. Can we doubt that, in comparison with any or all of these things God is greater, of more lasting interest, a more effective help to happiness?

A sound philosophy could be formed by directly answering these questions: Which is greater, the visible or the invisible? The material or the spiritual? The natural or the supernatural? The human or the divine? With what things am I most impressed? On what do I spend my thought and my time? I must find out if my chief concern is comfort, income, health, reputation. If so, I am obviously and profoundly wrong. Aid me, dear Master. It is to the greatest thing in the world that I should give most attention. And the greatest Thing is God!

FOUL outrages, deliberately perpetrated in a church, possess a sort of diabolical quality; the description of them has a peculiar power to shock, to disturb. The desecration of the temple at the hands of the money-changers angered Our Lord. Less than a half century later this same magnificent house of God was profaned and utterly destroyed by the Roman army. Yet for appalling horror neither of these sacrileges was comparable to what happened in the soul of Judas at the Last Supper. Nor were they comparable to the multiplied betrayals of Our Lord, which have occurred down through the years of Christian history in the hearts of those who profess to be His disciples.

Again we are driven to reflect on the frequency with which Jesus repeated that chiefly within the soul of man is the heavenly Father honored or dishonored. Not what comes in from without, but what goes out from within, makes a man unclean. External filth may well be regarded as a relatively weak and feeble symbol of the unimaginable, indescribable sacrilege which shocks the angels watching over the souls that Our Lord has redeemed. Yet strangely enough, we are more moved by external horrors than by the desecration of the inner temple of the soul, when God Himself is driven out of it with hate and cursing, with filthy words and savage blows.

Again I am led to look within. Again I am not content with what I see. I have been weak and feeble and disloyal, when attacked or allured by temptation. Once again, dear Lord, I ask forgiveness for the past. Once again I pledge in the future greater care, more constant vigilance—so that I may never again drive You away, as I have done so many times since first I received the blessed gift of grace!

Martha, Martha, Thou Art . . . Troubled About Many Things (Luke 10, 41)

"CAREFUL about too many things and too careful about almost everything"—this description fits a large number of persons. We may add that there are also persons who are careful about the wrong things—things sterile, unimportant, useless to a soul that hungers for happiness perfect and eternal. Persons of this type devote themselves to things that they know to be cheap and petty; things that leave a bad taste in the mouth and a sting in the heart; things that absorb time and care while God stands by unnoticed, and His poor suffer hardship and souls go astray.

Our Lord's words to Martha may be applied to all such. Can a man be called sane if he exhausts himself in the frantic pursuit of an object sure to be cast aside almost as soon as obtained; if he is deeply concerned, habitually anxious about what he knows possesses no real value? It seems incredible that any intelligent person could behave in this irrational fashion. Yet many of us do; and this happens because we refuse to measure the worth of things by God's standards; because instead of looking at the unworked harvest fields, we keep peering into a mirror; because we use a magnifying glass that enlarges trifles, not a telescope that lifts us to the stars.

If the coat fits me, I should put it on. If I will not look at things through God's eyes, then little wonder that I grow selfish, sad, unspiritual, morbid. Impress upon me, dear Master, the need of controlling my impulses and wishes. Help me to acquire a sense of proportion and balance. Let my most fervent desire be centered on perfect obedience to You. Let me set the activities of each day in the framework of Your Will. If I still need to have a Martha's hands, I will try to have a Mary's mind!

Mary Has Chosen the Better Part (Luke 10, 42)

IN THESE words Our Lord contrasted the quiet occupation of Mary, who sat at His feet, with that of her sister, Martha, who was "troubled about many things." The text is commonly interpreted as an approval of the contemplative vocation—a form of life which gives rise to much misunderstanding. Unbelievers and ill-instructed Catholics express amazement at the exaltation of the cloister. They ask what contemplatives can be doing with all their time. They protest against what they regard as the unconcern of the cloistered soul for men and women oustide the walls. They are mystified by an apparent divorce between the life of prayer on one hand and the life of social service on the other.

These protests show profound misunderstanding of the contemplative vocation, and indeed of the very nature of prayer. Persons who spend their days in silent worship are not anti-social, not egotists. They are deeply concerned with the welfare of their fellow creatures. Apostolic zeal is a conspicuous motif in their lives. They have not entered the cloister exclusively for their own sakes, but chiefly to consecrate days and nights to the worship of God and the service of mankind. Unless the whole Christian concept of life is wrong, the contemplative ideal is sound. Suffering multitudes will be helped by those who pray, as well as by those who labor; and much fruit will come from the prayer that contemplatives make for the labors of the missionary.

Teach me, dear Lord, to appreciate the immeasurable worth of prayer. I realize how mistaken I am, when I rely upon my own external activities more than upon communion with You. The approval You bestowed upon Mary shows how much value I must give to worship. I beg, therefore, that when I am called to commune with You in future, nothing and no one—absolutely nothing and absolutely no one—shall come as a veil before my mind, as a barrier to my will. Let the eyes of my soul be fixed upon You constantly; let the hands of my soul reach out and grope for Yours, Lord!

Sufficient for the Day Is Its Own Trouble (Matt. 6, 34)

THERE are some problems that cannot be answered, some problems that cannot be solved, some obstacles that cannot be passed. The sane man does not bang his head against a stone wall; the skilled commander knows when to retreat; the captain abandons a ship that is about to founder. All these examples teach the same lesson: we must not attempt, nor are we obliged to attempt, the impossible. This is a truth that some persons seem never willing to learn. The alternative to the learning of it may be exhaustion, perhaps a mental breakdown.

We find one type of person who is never ready to begin; another type who does not know when to stop. In both cases the individuals do not adjust themselves to reality. What possible advantage can come from refusing to conform to an inevitable law? It is surely always wise to accept what Providence permits. After having done our part, we should abandon ourselves and our world to Him. When we are not able to finish a task, we leave the rest of it in the hands of God. This is not indifference, or apathy, or cowardice; it is sanity. And sanity is part of sanctity.

By now, dear Master, I should have learned that my vocation is to follow You in all simplicity—nothing more. I do not have to succeed; I have only to attempt. In Your school of holiness there is no such thing as failure for the scholar who has good will. You wish us to proceed without anxiety, without strain, without waste. I shall not be called to account for having failed to solve a problem, if I have done my humble best to find the answer. I need not be concerned about the dead past, except to be grieved and sorrowful for my disloyalty to You. Neither need I worry about the unborn tomorrow, further than to resolve that the hours and days and weeks and years at my disposal shall be spent in simple obedience to Your Will.

Two Men Went Up to the Temple to Pray (Luke 18, 10)

THIS parable touches with everlasting splendor the figure of the humble publican. It bestows immortality of shame on the man who regards himself as better than his neighbor in the sight of God. Smugness and self-complacency are forever branded as characteristics hateful to God and to man. He who says to his neighbor, "I am holier than thou," is automatically classified as less holy. On the other hand, a soul that is deeply conscious of total dependence on God has already passed the first test for admission to the kingdom of Heaven.

We are drawn by the reading of this parable to contemplate two pictures—as in a gallery one might carefully study two paintings by some great master. Pointing to the representation of a man who measures the value and the interest of everything in the universe by its value and interest to himself, Our Lord says, "Here is the kind of human being I do not want My disciples to resemble." Pointing to the publican, He says, "If, like this man, you are aware of your own unworthiness, yet confident of God's mercy, you may already call yourself a Christian."

Once again then, I concentrate attention on the essential incompatibility of egotism and holiness. Once again, I note that to seek first place at table, to be hungry for respect, and honor and popularity to overlook the priceless value of meekness, is to invite exclusion from the kingdom of Heaven. I must try to discover in what respect I resemble the Pharisee. I must ask, how little do I resemble the publican? How much thought, how much effort, how much money, do I spend on myself? How much on God and my neighbor? Dear Lord, I look closely at the figure of the Pharisee; and I beg of You, do not let me be like that!

I Thank Thee That I Am Not Like the Rest of Men
(Luke 18, 11)

IF WE assume that this parable has no lesson for us simply because we do not use the same words that the Pharisee employed, we seem equivalently to be saying, "I thank Thee, O God, that I am not as this Pharisee." If I stick to the letter of Our Lord's teaching, I miss its spirit, I am like the Pharisee. If, on the other hand, I am more like the publican, this is not my own doing, but God's grace. It is something to be thankful for, not something to boast of. "What hast thou that thou hast not received? And if thou hast received it, why dost thou boast?"

Actually, many of us—although we do not realize it—bear a close resemblance to the Pharisee. Presumably he was quite unaware of his own faults and defects, forgetting the beam in his own eye, while marking the speck in his neighbor's. The Gospel does not affirm that the Pharisee was not as other men, but only that he said he was not. It may well be that he deserved to be placed in the front rank of extortioners, adulterers, unjust men; but by mere force of repition, he has convinced himself of his own moral superiority to those around him. Such things happen.

I must scrutinize this parable for points that could be applied to myself. Am I loud in rebuking the faults of others, yet ready to congratulate myself on my own good behavior? Do I speak glowingly of the joy of silence and the blessing of the peaceful life, while scattering seeds of hate around me wherever I go? Do I urge upon others the practice of a virtue which I imagine myself to possess, but against which I am constantly sinning? Lest I should really become a counterpart of the Pharisee, dear Lord, let me not rest satisfied with listening to Your words. Let me rather say now, "I begin to see in myself a certain resemblance to that self-centered man!"

O God, Be Merciful to Me the Sinner! (Luke 18, 13)

B E NOT deceived. God cannot err. He sees into the depths of every soul. He knows whether we lead lives as pure and good as we profess to lead. He knows whether our acts of virtue, our little kindnesses, our struggles against temptation, are to be attributed to love of Him, or to a self-satisfied, conceited spirit such as the Pharisee's.

When a man looks into his own heart, he should try to see it as God sees it. Perhaps he will find old, half-cured faults still lurking there. Perhaps he will come upon new faults that he has never suspected in himself —vanity, boastfulness, a tendency to harsh judgment, the habit of scandalous gossip, irreverence. If so, he should not be discouraged; but he should pray in the simple fashion of the publican: "O God, be merciful to me the sinner!" We must never imagine that God demands as a prerequisite for pardon anything more than a degree of humility and contrition which we may achieve with His help. God said to St. Paul, "My grace is sufficient for thee." He says the same to us.

Dear God, bestow upon me the precious gift of contrition which will fit me—even unworthy me—for the kingdom of Heaven. Help me to bear discomforts and humiliations and every other sort of burden, in the spirit of one who is glad to make even slow progress toward holiness. When I recall that the good thief and the bad thief reacted so differently to the same kind of suffering, I realize that day by day, and hour by hour, I am choosing Heaven or hell, accordingly as I am ready or unready to ask humbly for forgiveness of my sins. Let me decide now, definitely and finally, to live as one who has resolved, at all cost, to be a penitent!

He Who Humbles Himself Shall Be Exalted
(Luke 18, 14)

Few of the various practical directives formulated by Our Lord are more often ignored than His recommendation to be humble. Does not the behavior of the average Christian seem to imply an utter forgetfulness of, if not a total disbelief in, the validity of humility as a way of life? Proverbs, axioms, popular sayings, flatly contradict Our Lord's teaching in this respect; in pride the soul makes its last desperate stand against the influence of God's grace.

For this reason we are greatly enlightened and strengthened by remembering the words in which Our Lord offered Himself to us as a model. "Learn from Me, for I am meek and humble of heart." An artist is greatly aided by having before him a model that shows all the features of the masterpiece. So would be the builder and the engineer; so, too, the saint. A perfect model is especially helpful to the young artist, the apprentice architect, the spiritual novice, who are in the formative period of development. How stimulating to every man is the consciousness that he can grow Christ-like if he reproduces the pattern of conduct presented by Our Lord.

I thank You, dear Master, for the precious gift bestowed upon me when You offered Yourself as a model. I will try to make daily use of this aid. Distasteful as humility is to me, I will, at Your bidding, try to become humble. I know that insofar as I make progress in the acquiring of this quality—so disliked by men, so dear to God—I shall be moving toward the fulfillment of my vocation, which is to be exalted to the company of those who worship You eternally in Heaven!

In This Manner . . . Shall You Pray (Matt. 6, 9)

NOT IN this passage only, but in many other parts of the Gospel also, we find Our Lord teaching us the art of prayer. Over and over again He conveys the tone, the shading, the suggestion of the unique relationship that connected the Father in Heaven with His beloved Son here upon earth. Our knowledge of that relationship illuminates the subject of prayer amazingly. And we find still another precious lesson on prayer in the union with God which our Lady possessed—a perfect example of the union desired by all the other saints, but not attained by them in this life completely or continuously.

Thinking of these things, I begin to see new meaning in the simple definition of prayer as a lifting up of the mind and will to God. This definition indicates that in the measure that I renounce all that hinders, and cultivate all that promotes the concentrating of my mind and will on God; and that in the measure I correspond with the grace which enables me at least dimly to see, and at least imperfectly to grasp, the ever-present God; in that same measure can I be said really to pray. Obviously whatever helps to unite us with God is an aid to prayer. Whatever hinders it should—so far as the interests of prayer are concerned—be set aside.

Help me, dear Lord, to commune with You ever more intensely, ever more continually. Move me to pay the necessary price of setting aside distractions, of renouncing every desire that does not harmonize with Your Will. It is, I see, only in the fixing of my attention on You and in the harmonizing of my will with Yours, that I shall achieve virtue in this life and blessedness in the life to come. This then, I long for above everything else. This I beg of You as the most desirable of all gifts!

10th WEEK AFTER PENTECOST—FRIDAY
The Father Also Seeks Such to Worship Him
(John 4, 23)

PRAYER is communion with God. It has been compared to the lifeblood that keeps body and soul together, to the oxygen without which man cannot live, to the current which makes an electric bulb incandescent. Cut the arteries, shut off the oxygen, throw open the switch; and we have death and darkness, symbol of a soul that has abandoned prayer. Dependent upon its own resources, it ceases to live.

Persons who strive for spiritual progress must sooner or later face the conflicting claims of work and prayer. Although no identical formula can be applied to all souls, there is a rule quite sufficient for practical purposes: work as if everything depended on self; pray as if everything depended on God. This leaves the theoretical problem unsolved, yet carries home the conviction that prayer is certainly not less important than work. While it is true that both are indispensable, it is also true that if one had to be sacrificed, work and not prayer should go. A man would be wrong to imagine that he might lawfully labor so hard as to leave no time or strength for prayer.

Give me, dear Lord, proper appreciation of that habit of communion with the Father, which is dearer to the saints than life itself. Make me wise enough and strong enough to put aside anything that interferes with the cultivation of this habit. Like many another soul, I am often drawn away from God's Presence by the appeal of work which promises large rewards in consolation and in honor; and I know that unless I curb my eagerness sufficiently to find time for quiet communion and inner worship, I shall not be conforming to the pattern of life which You established for Your disciples. The Father who calls laborers into the vineyard, also seeks for souls to adore Him. I have a place among these worshipers. May it not be left empty!

I Confess to Thee Heavenly Father (Matt. 11, 25)

To "confess" means to affirm one's faith and trust, to acknowledge, to recognize, to give praise. The word reminds us that Our Lord's prayer often took the form of simple worship, of acknowledging the heavenly Father for what He truly is—the infinitely perfect One, on whom we depend for all we have, to whom we pay tribute by offering all we ever can have, or ever can be. When a man stands before God and makes a complete offering of himself, his wishes and desires, his hopes and fears, his faculties, and his possessions, then he is "confessing." His prayer is perfect when it is free of all self-consideration, calculation, reservation. It passes the final test when the one who prays is faithful to his "confession" to the end of life.

In all these respects Our Lord was perfect; and so His prayer was that perfect prayer upon which we model our own. His prayer stimulates, guides, assists us. Thus we produce ever-changing reflections of infinite wisdom and infinite goodness in our own limited, finite souls. As God's creative activity is reflected in the trees of the forest that fascinate us with their ever varying displays of hue and color, so Our Lord's prayer is echoed and repeated in the timid, fearful prayer of the newly converted sinner, in the eager, bold, soaring aspiration of the saint.

The stars, the sea, the everlasting hills, the forest with its leaves like "myriad hands upturned in prayer," will remind me to "confess" Your power and knowledge and goodness, dear Lord. Make me often—at least for a moment—acutely conscious of Your Presence, as was the poet who wrote:

"Yet ever and anon a trumpet sounds
From the hid battlements of Eternity;
Those shaken mists a space unsettle, then
Round the half-glimpsed turrets slowly wash again."

11th WEEK AFTER PENTECOST—SUNDAY
Be Thou Opened (Mark 7, 34)

WITH these words Our Lord restored hearing and speech to one deaf and dumb. When we come upon a man deprived of sight, of hearing, or of any other faculty, we may well be moved to a consideration of the various ways in which we commonly misuse God's gifts. We ask ourselves the question: Why is it that we are able to hear and see, whereas others remain deaf and blind? Some high purpose God must have had, when He gave us these gifts; and we shall be wise if we consider whether or not we are using them in accord with that purpose. Not merely must we keep from misusing them; we must employ them positively in His service. The servant who buried his talent in the ground was guilty only of negative wrongdoing; yet he was punished.

Negligence in using God's gifts is sinful. Even worse than negligence is misuse. Have I not at times turned God's gifts against Him, and against His children? When the final balance is struck, will the world be better because I have lived in it? Or may it be that, on the whole, the interests of God and man would have been better served had I never been born?

What a terrifying thought this is! Bad enough, dear Lord, that I should have misused many opportunities of using my gift of speech to please You, to help my neighbor, to benefit my own soul. Far worse that I have so misused it as to hurt You and my neighbor and myself. Shock me then into a realization that I must set about the correcting of my habitual failures; that I must take definite steps to avoid sins of the tongue, and to employ my power of speech in the practice of kindness and zeal and prayer. What a precious privilege it is to be able to further Your plans, to increase the merits that You have made it possible for me to acquire, to help bring stray souls back to You. This is my divine vocation. Let me resolve to be true to it.

Our Father Who Art in Heaven, Hallowed Be Thy Name (Matt. 6, 9)

To THOSE of us who are accustomed to think of prayer as a means of obtaining aid from the heavenly Father, the opening words of the Lord's Prayer are particularly illuminating. For these words impress us with the rule that the first concern of the soul at prayer is not its own needs, but the honoring of God's Name. As we turn to Our Father to give expression to our deep desires, our first request should be that He may receive His due, that He may be honored, worshiped, glorified by all men, everywhere, always.

It is not a meaningless, superfluous desire to which we thus give expression; for God has not always received His due from those exalted creatures made in His image, whose high destiny it is to give Him glory. Some of them have been loyal, but not all. Some have forgotten Him; some have distrusted Him; some have rebelled against Him. In one way or another men, and angels too, have fallen far short of the end for which they are created. Inevitably then, the soul that is sensitively acute, finely attuned to the Divine Will, aware of what the order of the universe demands, will turn away from the vision of human sin and human selfishness with an irresistible longing to have things put right; to have the Creator again recognized as supreme; to have His goodness appreciated by His creatures and His Name hallowed.

I should, and I must, contribute more generously, more faithfully, to God's honor. I must remember His goodness and His greatness, realize my dependence on Him, recognize Him as the Giver of all good things ever possessed by me or any creature—and wish that all men may do the same. All human beings belong to God. May all of them become holy, with attention fixed on God like the blessed in Heaven or contemplative souls on earth, and with wills perfectly adjusted to His Will. May I strive everlastingly to have it thus in the souls of all, but in my own soul first. On my lips, in my heart, by my deeds—Hallowed be Thy Name!

Thy Kingdom Come (Matt. 6, 10)

To SAY "Thy kingdom come" implies a desire, a resolution. It means that we wish for the coming of the kingdom. We profess to support the principles on which that kingdom is founded—meekness, truth-telling, fair play, respect for men, reverence for God—always and everywhere at whatever cost. We undertake to speed its coming, in so far as we may. We set ourselves against the forces that oppose its coming—selfishness, injustice, uncharity, lies.

Our Lord's prayer, then, re-echoes the ideals proclaimed in the Sermon on the Mount. The kingdom of God is the kingdom of Light. Justice reigns there; and truth; and joy. All is in order—as it should be. There shall be no sorrow, no weeping, no want, no fear. Perfect freedom will prevail—the liberty of the children of God. There, men cannot but love good and avoid evil.

All this reminds me of serious defects of speech and conduct which make me look very unlike a citizen of the kingdom of God. These defects point like fingers at changes that must be made in my daily routine—drastic changes. I fail to conform to the pattern deeply impressed upon my conscience. What about my preference for self at the expense of justice? Dear Lord, help me to acquire the habit of thinking first of others, and of myself last; help me to acquire the habit of speaking without equivocation, even though it may bring upon me discomforts and humiliations—which of course can be very profitable to my soul. Do not let me forget how greatly I must improve if I am to say sincerely, "Thy kingdom come!" I must resolve to repeat this prayer many times each day, keeping in mind each time that it commits me to wholehearted acceptance of all Our Lord's ideals, and implies firm determination to persist in the effort to realize them.

11th WEEK AFTER PENTECOST—WEDNESDAY
Thy Will Be Done (Matt. 6, 10)

THIS perfect prayer, this comprehensive rule of life, was anticipated in our Blessed Lady's answer to Gabriel: "Be it done to me according to Thy word!" It has been repeated countless times in moments of agonizing pain or of tragic bereavement, by humble, unknown saints—some of whom we ourselves may have looked upon in their sorrow. Patient, prayerful souls are these —to whom we listen, or of whom we think in reverent admiration. They were wholehearted and self-forgetting in their abandonment to the Will of God. And the memory of them still has power to move us, after ten or twenty or fifty years.

Submission to the divine Will is necessarily included —at least by implication—in any petition made in the name of Christ. It formed part of His own prayer when, in the Garden of Gethsemane, He besought relief—but only on condition that this relief should be according to the heavenly Father's Will. On many occasions, Our Lord encourages us to ask for things we need, or seem to need, and to ask with the spontaneous readiness of a child; but He wishes us not to insist upon our own preference; for we have little wisdom, little foresight.

Therefore, dear Lord, I will endeavor always to pray in accord with Your teaching. I will try gladly to substitute Your Will for my wishes and decisions. I know that my best laid plans often prove to be unwise and ineffective. I know that what You choose for me is dictated by Your wisdom, Your love. And I know that You will give me either the gift I ask for, or something that eventually I shall recognize to be far better. May it be done unto me, then, according to Thy word in every least respect —every day and every hour. Never can I hope to reach a higher level of achievement or of happiness than that which is represented by the acceptance of Your Will.

Give Us This Day Our Daily Bread (Matt. 6, 11)

IT IS comforting to know that Our Lord not only allows but also urges us to ask for food to sustain our bodily life. In bidding us pray for our daily bread, He lays down the broad foundation on which we may base a sane and wisely balanced way of life. Man is a dual creature, not a disembodied spirit; the body no less than the soul came from God, and must be cared for and preserved by man. The gifts of the material order are good gifts. We recognize them as coming from God; we ask Him to bestow them upon us, to satisfy our daily needs. We make this part of our prayer.

Not in name alone are we children of the Father. Not idly does Christ tell us that the very hairs of our heads are numbered. It is He who has given us life; and it is He who gives us the things that sustain life—food, drink, shelter. To take this as literally true; to accept every gift of the material order as sent by God; to ask for them in our need and to use them in right order and proportion —all this means living according to the Will of God and in harmony with the spiritual teaching of Our Lord who taught us to say, "Our Father who art in heaven,... give us this day our daily bread."

May I always see clearly the close connection between material and spiritual things. May I never forget that this body of mine is a gift from God who wills me to care for it with all reverence. Food and drink and every other material good, I may seek and even pray for; but I must always employ these and all other gifts in strict harmony with God's plan. I must not overeat, nor overdrink, nor work too hard, nor relax too much. I see, dear Master, how greatly I shall gain if I combine dependence on You with the habit of stern self-control. Aid me to do this.

Forgive Us Our Debts As We . . . Forgive (Matt. 6, 12)

RECIPROCITY is a policy which commends itself to all who possess the normal sense of justice. Even when we stand on the low level of elementary decency, we are accustomed to rebuke sternly persons who demand, but never allow, concessions. Anyone who takes without giving, who asks but never offers, provokes immediate and strong disapproval. Instinctively we blame the use of this double standard in human relationships. We know it will lead to situations confused, chaotic, saturated with dangerous possibilities in social, in commercial, in political life.

The selection of a disinterested outsider as arbiter is imposed upon us by custom and also usually by law. We laugh at the idea of applying the word "just" to a court in which either a complainant or a defendant is judge. It has become a commonplace in our usage to exclude a man from acting as referee or sitting on a jury in a case which involves his interests. This usage has come as the result of bitter experience. We have enshrined our wisdom in proverbs, "No one is a judge in his own case." "Sauce for the goose, sauce for the gander." "Live and let live." Yet comparatively few persons see clearly the implications of the principle of fair play which all so loudly proclaim.

What about my procedure in the inner court of conscience? Am I fair? Am I just? Do I follow the same rules in granting, as in seeking, pardon? Dear Lord, if I could become in this respect impersonal, what a blessing it would be for me and for those with whom I come in daily contact. I would not then readily ask pardon for my offenses against You, unless I were equally ready to grant pardon to those who offend me. Neither would I quite so glibly recite these words You taught me to say about forgiving others; and in practice I would habitually forgive others as I hope to be forgiven.

Lead Us Not Into Temptation (Matt. 6, 13)

THE SOUL who makes this prayer thereby professes the desire to avoid temptation—a desire which is of the very essence of holiness. Not to avoid temptation —in so far as it is reasonably avoidable—is to play with fire, a hazardous sort of activity, little favored by men who have set their wills on God. Absorbed with the idea of advancing steadily toward Heaven, they turn away from occasions of sin, fearing to tread where fools rush in—the fools who so easily and frequently become actual sinners under the pressure of temptation.

If we analyze the motives which impel us to trifle with temptation, we find in ourselves an unwillingness to put God's interests first. Other aims have priority over the doing of His Will and the carrying out of His plan. Most frequently these other aims involve self-indulgence and vanity. We seek either pleasure for ourselves or approval from others. God comes last.

Hence Christ bids us pray against temptation, bids us guard against the subtle infiltration of selfishness. There must be no yielding to envy which suggests that others have an easier time than I, to sloth which bids me postpone my effort until tomorrow. I must not let myself be hampered by my possessions; I must not engage in gossip, nor let myself be distracted by worldly interests. There must be less indulgence, more austerity, less talk and entertainment, more prayer and communion. The longing for excitement and pleasure is no justification for running the risk of spiritual disaster. On the tree of my will, God will look for nothing but good fruit. May it be there and ready for Your taking, dear Lord.

12th WEEK AFTER PENTECOST—SUNDAY
Thou Hast Answered Rightly (Luke 10, 28)

A LAWYER had questioned Our Lord, wondering if there were not some novel step to be taken, some new place to visit, some person to consult in order to be saved. Jesus brought out the answer by leading the lawyer to affirm the everlasting truth that lies at the basis of all religion: "Thou shalt love the Lord thy God with thy whole heart, and with thy whole soul, and with thy whole strength, and with thy whole mind; and thy neighbor as thyself." Our Lord's approval of this answer obviates the need of further questioning by us, or by anyone.

Love is "the fulfilling of the law." With love, every duty is accomplished; without it, none. The divine law demands simply that one should live out all that is implied in this fundamental commitment— an obligation that cannot be misunderstood, that admits of no escape no excuse. When we love as we should, we consecrate all our strength to making God's interests supreme; and we place our neighbor before ourselves.

If I could but make this ideal my own! If I could but reflect in my conduct, as the saints have done, the implications of the faith which is mine as well as theirs! For one blessed moment at least, I see now what the old mystic saw centuries ago when he wrote in *Praise of Love*: "Tell me, O heart of man, wouldst thou prefer to rejoice always in this world, or always to be with God? Whichever pleaseth thee best, that choose. . . . Love, then, that thou mayst be able to choose; love more fervently that thou mayst be able to choose more happily; love God, that thou mayst be able to choose God For it is by loving that thou dost choose."

12th WEEK AFTER PENTECOST—MONDAY
A Certain Samaritan . . . Took Care of Him
(Luke 10, 34)

THE parable of the Good Samaritan is short, picturesque, persuasive. It is not merely the clarifying of an ideal; it is the proclamation of divine law. The way the Samaritan behaved when he came upon the helpless, wounded stranger, is the way that you and I and every man must behave if we are to be disciples of Christ, in deed as well as in word.

Standing out so plain in Our Lord's teaching as to be almost startling, is the indissoluble connection between love of God and love of man. The soul that truly loves is like God; and resemblance to God means that hatred is excluded—a point that must be carefully considered by any nominal Christian who keeps aversion in his heart, a scowl on his brow, bitter words on his tongue. Even more! Resemblance to God means that, like Him, we include all men in our affectionate care. It is not a question of tolerating; our obligation binds us to be considerate and gentle and helpful toward all with whom we come in contact. From this obligation of serving, we are not excused even when such service is distasteful and burdensome to ourselves.

What shall guide me in my attempt to discover whether or not I really love God, whether or not I am in truth a disciple of Christ? Unquestionably, the proper test is my attitude toward my neighbor. From the story of the Samaritan, I acquire a new sense of what Christ meant by love. It is not the name we have but the deed we do that avails for salvation before God. Let me try to realize this; let me try to be a Christian after the heart of Christ. As I have been brought to understand that the blessing of God rested on the Samaritan who showed mercy and kindness, let me beat myself into shape and act like him. The things that I should do this day or this week will be easy to discover if I look around.

12th WEEK AFTER PENTECOST—TUESDAY
Do This and Thou Shalt Live (Luke 10, 28)

THESE words guarantee Heaven on the fulfillment of one condition. If I love God and my neighbor, I shall possess eternal life. But that condition is high, heroic, difficult of achievement. The love of which Our Lord speaks is in sharp contrast to the motion of love commonly entertained by the world—the love that provides material for the sensational press, the scandal sheets, the popular fiction.

It is a common practice of men when they face an extremely burdensome obligation, to explain it away, translate it into a more comfortable equivalent, settle for a short rather than a long range policy. They yield to that inclination which disposes us to keep on the beaten track or stay at home; they succumb to the pressure of the crowd; they roll along in a rut rather than carry a heavy load over untrodden fields. Thus does the momentum of early enthusiasm gradually slow down; and the promise of flaming youth fades into the commonplace mediocrity of dull middle age.

Those who have read the story of Your life and pondered Your teaching, dear Lord, cannot be mistaken about the true nature of the love which You exact from Your disciples. It cannot be confused with the eager desire of sensual gratification, the passionate hunger that so easily turns into jealousy and hate. That false notion is accepted by persons around me whose conduct I observe and whose words I hear. Possibly they have some excuse for their mistake, which seems to blaspheme the name of love. But there can be no excuse for me. Let me not shut my ears to Your teaching, nor turn away from the sight of Your example. Let me keep it stamped upon my memory. This will require all my best effort; but if I am to become able to love, I must be strong to suffer and constant to persevere.

Which of These . . . Proved Himself Neighbor?
(Luke 10, 36)

OUR Lord's question evoked the definition of a neighbor as one who shows mercy. A neighbor is one who thinks first not of self but of others, noting their needs, commiserating their misfortunes, changing plans even to the extent of breaking up a journey, postponing serious business, spending time and money upon unfortunate strangers. A neighbor befriends the unknown victim of misfortune, and instantly bestows on him the help of which he stands in need. This type of man symbolizes charity. He embodies the affection that knits men togther in the bonds of lasting friendship, blessing both "him that gives and him that takes." This is the kind of neighbor we all would like to have. This is the kind of neighbor we all must try to be.

There is no possibility of my pursuing the ideal presented to me in the parable of the Good Samaritan, unless I am prepared to pay a price. There is no sense in my repeating the excuses that come to my lips so quickly, little use in saying "no one does this"; or "everyone is doing that"; or "people won't like my acting this way"; or "I may be misunderstood"; or "I do not want to pose as generous"; or "this man has done nothing for me"; or "I do not want to pretend to have sympathy that I do not feel." A master of novices once playfully said to a pupil, "When you do not feel attracted to your neighbor, you had better practice a little pious dissimulation."

If I am to overcome the difficulties that spring from original sin, and if I am to conquer grave temptations, I need Your help, dear Lord. Let me face the situation frankly. You have set the ideal before me. And I must decide whether I am bent on pleasing You by pursuing this ideal, or bent on pleasing myself.

I Have Given You An Example (John 13, 15)

THE parable of the Good Samaritan has been impressed indelibly on the Christian imagination. Nor has it been a picture merely. It may be compared to ever-fruitful seed from which a harvest comes in every period of Christian history. The spirit of Christ, illustrated by the story of the Good Samaritan, has constantly reappeared both in the organized activities of religious communities and in the heroic lives of countless individuals.

Among the examples on which we may profitably dwell is the career of St. Peter Claver, Spanish by birth and Jesuit missionary by profession, who died almost three hundred years ago, after having devoted most of his life to serve unhappy slaves brought from Africa to South America. Ministering to the physical and spiritual needs of these vermin-infested, disease-ridden men and women, amid circumstances too nauseating for us even to dwell upon, he brought more than a quarter of of a million of them to baptism during his forty years of labor. How deep his faith, how strong his courage must have been to brave not only discomfort and danger, but also widespread disapproval, amid such conditions as these.

Thinking of Peter Claver and of many others like him, I confess, dear Lord, that I am at first baffled and dismayed. They translated into action the ideals of charity which You pointed out as proper for Your disciples. I, on the other hand, usually try to explain Your words away and to devise for myself a rule of life more practical, less uncomfortable. Now, however, I am ashamed of my weakness, my sloth, my lack of courage. I realize I must not substitute some other way for the way You pointed out to Your disciples. I will not yield to that temptation, if for no other reason, then for this—one who does not love and serve cannot resemble You.

12th WEEK AFTER PENTECOST—FRIDAY
Take Heed . . . How You Hear (Luke 8 ,18)

THESE words might well have been addressd to the lawyer who had asked a question, the answer to which he himself already knew. A good many of us are like this lawyer; for often by way of postponing a summons to action, we propose unnecessary and even unanswerable questions. There is an ignorance which is culpable, a blindness which is wilful; and these do not provide a valid excuse for delaying, or refusing, to do our duty. If we are wilfully ignorant, we are blameworthy. There are none so blind as those who will not see.

The attitude of the Good Samaritan offers a pointed contrast to that of the lawyer. The Samaritan did not waste time asking questions. He saw at once what was required; he spent effort and time and money; he "followed through," providing not only for the immediate need of the unfortunate traveler, but also for the future. The Samaritan stands out not only as a contrast to the lawyer, but also as a model for men and women to imitate whenever there is an opportunity to help someone in great need.

As I bring these things to mind, I recognize that they are old, familiar truths—lessons which I seem to have learned only to forget. So much of the truth that You have taught me, dear Lord, has passed completely out of memory—as I see the instant I scrutinize my conduct carefully. I know there is good ground for alarm if the reproaches of conscience, once loud enough to be easily heard, have faded to a mere whisper, because they are consistently disregarded. Hidden away in the recesses of my memory are many teachings, clearly formulated by You and confirmed by my own bitter experience. Help me to bring these to the foreground of my consciousness. Let me not forget what I have been taught.

The Spirit Indeed Is Willing, But the Flesh Is Weak
(Matt. 26, 41)

MODERN psychiatry—source of both good and evil—has this to its credit, that it emphasizes the enormous influence of early experiences upon the adult character. The knowledge of this profound relationship between youth and maturity is not new. We find it expressed in proverbs—"The child is father to the man"; "As the twig is bent the tree's inclined." But the fact is more strongly emphasized and given wider circulation than before; it is subjected to more careful study. We are led to observe the various kinds of pressure to which the child is subjected, the formal and informal discipline undergone, the habits that take root during the first plastic period of development.

We thus discover fresh significance in those ancient terms and phrases which contrast the lower and the higher self, the old man and the new, the sensual and the spiritual nature. We see in clearer light the commonly forgotten truth that man is an animal. We note the similarity between the play of infants and the play of kittens or puppies; and we realize the immense significance of the prerational years, which formed our habit of acting on the single motive of seeking pleasure and avoiding pain. The thrusting up of these early habits into the higher level of later rational behavior gives rise to the conflict which torments the wisest and the strongest and the best of men. St. Paul records his anguish of spirit at willing, but not doing, good; at rejecting, yet doing, evil.

Dear Lord, You have made plain to me, that in order to grow strong I must school myself in self-denial. I must accustom myself to bearing crosses, little or great, which Your Providence allows to be placed upon my shoulders. I must attempt to share the spirit and imitate the conduct of the saints. So acting, I may hope, with the help of Your grace, to build up habits of doing my duty and obeying Your Will, no matter how weak the flesh may be, no matter how loud is the protest of the body at being forced to endure discomfort or pain.

Where Are the Nine? (Luke 17, 17)

THIS reproach reminds us that of the ten lepers who had been cleansed only one returned to thank Our Lord. It requires little effort for us to picture the discomfort, misery, suffering, shame, which had been the daily lot of these men. Now in an instant life takes on a new color. Hope returns. They will enjoy the blessings possessed by other normal persons; they will share the give and take of friendship.

We might reasonably expect that a flood of gratitude would well up in the soul of a person rescued from so miserable a fate and restored to so comforting a prospect. Yet, in every case but one, the lepers who had been healed proved to be inappreciative. Our condemnation of the ungrateful lepers may well become the measure of our own self-reproach. For, when we begin to compare ourselves with them, it seems quite obvious that most of us are more like the nine who never came back, than like the one who returned.

I am thus impelled to think of Your unending goodness to me, dear Lord. It will be well for me to take pencil and paper and set about making at least a partial list of the blessings I have received from Your hands. At once I see that the number is overwhelming, dismaying. But at any rate I can make a start at listing the proofs of Your goodness to me; and I can make these proofs the starting point of a prayer of gratitude. And I can keep on adding to the list, day by day, as my memory sharpens and my imagination grows more vivid. I do realize, dear Lord and Master, that I cannot thank You too much and too often for what You have done; and I had better begin to discharge my obligation, at least in part, this very instant.

Has No One Been Found to Return . . . Except This Foreigner? (Luke 17, 18)

IT SEEMS like a cynical comment on human nature to say that we pray most fervently when we are asking for something. One would like to believe that a normal instinct of decency and a proper sense of proportion would move men to thank God for favors received as earnestly as they ask for favors desired. But experience shows that the average recipient of God's gifts is at least as ready to forget His goodness as the nine lepers were.

To be sure, there are many people who do give evidence of their thankfulness to God. We know that prayers are lifted up, Masses offered, altars and churches erected, tablets displayed on walls as evidences of grateful appreciation. Yet those who do these things are only a small proportion of the vast number who have received rich gifts. Thinking of the ten lepers who were cleansed and of the one who returned, we are moved to speculate if persons who offer prayers of thanksgiving are even one-tenth as numerous as persons who offer prayers of petition.

I feel quite sure that I am among those who, like the nine ungrateful lepers, give no evidence of gratitude for blessings received—not even for one-tenth of them. Like many others, I accept as a matter of course gifts for which countless multitudes of my fellow creatures would be thankful. Hundreds of thousands would be unspeakably grateful if they could rise to their feet and walk, if they were sheltered, and clothed, and fed, as I am. With the thought of Your goodness thus forced upon me, dear Lord, I turn to You now asking You to aid me to thank You in becoming fashion. Let me give expression to my thankfulness not only in words but by faithful service, too.

Of Everyone to Whom Much Has Been Given, Much Will Be Required (Luke 12, 48)

SOME OF us seem to possess no proper sense of values until we have encountered misfortune. When a treasure has been stolen we begin to prize it as never before. We appreciate water, air, food, health, friendship, after we have suffered at least a partial loss of them—thus with the gifts of sight and hearing. Only when facing the prospect of losing them, do we realize how great a blessing are these faculties which hitherto we have taken as a matter of course.

Most of us are like this with regard to our spiritual blessings, too. We have been set a little lower than the angels; in some respects we have been even more favored than they. Yet we have only a dim perception of God's goodness; and we manifest our gratitude in feeble, inadequate fashion. Those who are profoundly and continually grateful, and who make an earnest effort to repay their divine Benefactor by prayers and by good deeds as well—these form a small minority.

Among the grateful few I am not included. If my heart were right and my spiritual vision keen, then I would be singing a song of thanksgiving every waking hour of my life; and I would be grateful not only for gifts that bring joy and peace and consolation, but for discomfort and hardship as well. For, to one who looks at life through Your eyes, dear Lord, nothing is clearer than the precious value of the Cross. Much can be gained by effort and by struggle—the sailor's sight is keen, the porter's back is strong, the mountaineer is sturdy. On the other hand, uninterrupted ease is commonly associated with self-indulgence, and moral feebleness. Help me then, dear Lord, to appreciate the uses of adversity, the wisdom of trusting You in the dark. I will receive gratefully whatever comes from Your hand.

If These Keep Silence, the Stones Will Cry Out
(Luke 19, 40)

IT WOULD be an interesting experiment to question two or three good people on their interpretation of these words of Our Lord. They were spoken, we may recall, when the Pharisees asked the Master to rebuke the disciples for rejoicing over the miracles they had seen. Instead of rebuking, He justified them; and at the same time He provided you and me with material for serious consideration. For the real point of His reproach touches everyone of us who fails to bear witness to what God has done in this world of ours.

The rule of action suggested in the text, does not call upon us to make ourselves annoying to others; there must be discretion in our zeal for the glory of God and for the spread of truth. But Our Lord sharply reproaches persons who, while enjoying the privileges of the true faith, remain silent, tongue-tied, inactive—who make no move toward enlightening and assisting their neighbors. Not infrequently someone outside the Church is heard to ask, "Why are Catholics reluctant to communicate the knowledge of their splendid heritage?" This seems to be a question to which there is no satisfactory and creditable reply.

Although I have not been entirely silent, I know well I have not been as zealous as I could have been in the spreading of the truth. Please God, I will develop new enthusiasm for the sharing of God's gifts; and I will urge those whom I can influence to enroll themselves in the spiritual army that carries on this modern crusade. If I bear witness to Your goodness, dear Lord, my words may enlighten many hitherto uninformed. If I bear witness, many, too timid to make the first step alone, will come forward because of this encouragement. Let me no longer keep silence, then, but speak so that I may help to bring everlasting happiness to souls hitherto empty of joy.

FROM time to time, newspapers report a large but unexpected bequest, left by a rich man to one who had been kind to him. Perhaps for years, or perhaps only during the last days of life; perhaps in heroic fashion, or perhaps in a minor, unnoticed way he had been served; and the good deed was forgotten entirely by the one who did it. The benefactor is quite surprised to find himself remembered. Thus, in Our Lord's parable of the Judgment, the souls about to enter heaven were amazed at being rewarded for kind deeds which they had quite forgotten.

Gratitude is characteristic of noble spirits; and we can be quite sure that any service to God will be rewarded a hundredfold. This is the counterpart of that other truth which we should keep constantly in mind, namely, that we can never possibly profit by disobeying or by forgetting God. To be sure, there are men who profess to be, on the one hand, wholly free from fear about the consequences of their deeds and, on the other hand, completely insensitive to anything like a prospect of reward. But it is normal and human to be motivated by fear of loss and expectancy of profit. And we surely act more easily and more smoothly, and encounter fewer emotional obstacles when we are doing something that promises to bring joy, not grief.

Quite humbly, dear Lord, I confess that it is easier for me to serve You when I remember Your promise to leave nothing done for You unrewarded. Keep me ever conscious that the things I most desire are sure to be lost if I do not get them from You. Help me to have clear before my mind the truth that, in the long run, nothing but goodness will pay. Then, and then only, will the prospect of future joy, certain and unending, shine upon my course as a beacon light. I will fix my eyes on You as the center of the world in which I belong, and outside of which I cannot be at peace. Your interests are always on the same side as mine. May I see this as clearly in every moment of temptation as I see it now!

Deliver Us from Evil (Matt. 6, 13)

OFTEN men speak of "what might have been." And usually they refer to gifts, blessings, opportunities, which would have brought large measure of contentment and happiness. However, there is another side to this. The "might have been" should include perils and misfortunes happily escaped. One should think not only of the good that was never gained, but also of the suffering that was never undergone. We might have been—like so many others—undernourished, poorly educated, brought up with no religious training. We might have been cut off in youth; or died while out of God's friendship. We might have missed certain rich opportunities that have been profitably utilized. It is good to learn from others and to see in many respects how much more fortunate we are. This is the kind of lesson one might learn during a visit to a hospital, or even to a jail.

There have been near accidents, never known, that I have escaped — collisions, for example. Others were trapped in that train wreck, or that fire—why not I? I have seen persons living under handicaps, physical and mental, which make it difficult for me to look at them without a surge of pity. Why am I not like them?

I bring before my mind big or little things of this sort, and I see how they may be made a theme of prayer. Let me be uninterruptedly grateful, then, both for blessings bestowed on me and for the fact that I have escaped so many dangers. I think now of all the good gifts I might have missed which mean so much to me— my training, my faith, my friends, good books, sermons, helpful teachers and confessors. As I think of the pardon so generously and so frequently given me, I remember Your words, dear Lord, "The more one has been forgiven, the more one loves."

If Thy Eye Be Sound (Matt. 6, 22)

A PROVERB bids us "Beware the man of one book." It implies that if we concentrate on one object we shall probably accomplish more than we could accomplish by scattering our energies far and wide. This is equivalent to saying that, especially in important matters, it is wise to do one thing at a time. If our supply of energy is limited—as invariably it is—and if we undertake more than prudence dictates, everything will be wasted and no one will be satisfied. This is the fatal blunder that generals try to avoid.

True, there is danger of extravagance. One does not put all the eggs in one basket. Yet neither should one try to put one egg in several baskets—which is precisely the mistake that some of us repeatedly make. We have time, grace, sufficient to do one thing well; but we are not content to limit ourselves to the task assigned by God. We strain. We are overcome by exhaustion. Then we sit down with our task half done; and it is never completed.

I see that the proper treatment for the illness from which I suffer is the cultivation of simplicity. I perceive how much egotism there is in my eagerness. I know, dear Lord, that if I were concerned merely with the doing of Your Will, I would not be hurried as I am, nor distracted by a jarring multitude of interests pulling me hither and thither, and driving me to do many things poorly, nothing well. Help me to cultivate simplicity. Teach me to let others have their full share of honorable employment and due notice. I must remember that "turn about is fair play." I must rejoice when others get what seem to be pleasanter or more honorable assignments than mine. I must even be glad when they succeed where I have failed.

You Cannot Serve God and Mammon (Matt. 6, 24)

WE ARE all potential traitors. The lower self, the old Adam, the flesh that lusts against the spirit, exerts powerful pressure upon the will. Who will guarantee successful resistance? The fact is we are pulled in different directions by divergent motives; and most men will shift position, modify principles, allow exceptions when comfort, self-esteem or popularity is threatened. Those of us who—openly or secretly—have a double allegiance must sooner or later face a "showdown." If we are to remain faithful to Our Lord and keep free from sin, we must have special help, more than ordinary grace.

Little wonder, then, that Our Lord so often tells us to simplify and strengthen our loyalties. One reason why there are so few saints is that few persons make up their minds finally and definitely to serve God only, at whatever cost; and of these few still fewer persist. We have to set aside many things which are legitimate in themselves, simply because we have not time and energy enough for them and for Our Lord. If a man is to be with Him at all, he must be with Him wholeheartedly. If not with Him wholeheartedly, he is equivalently against Him. Since we cannot serve two masters, we had better decide now who is our real master, and what he wants us to do.

Dear Lord, I choose You for my one and only Master. Assign my work and give such payment as You think best, and when You choose. The prayer of the liturgy reminds us that without Your help no one can hope to keep from falling. Aid me and all Your other children, then, to avoid all things hurtful; and lead us to all things profitable for salvation. May the sacraments purify us and strengthen us; and may You enable us to attain the everlasting reward that You have promised to those who remain faithful!

Do Not Be Anxious . . . About Tomorrow (Matt. 6, 34)

IN THE natural law there is a system to which a man must accommodate himself if he wishes to live. Care for one's life—the instinct of self-preservation—is called nature's first law; yet Christ's precept seems to run counter to it. It actually runs counter, however, only in so far as it prohibits *undue* concern for our physical welfare. And the reason for the prohibition is that our solicitude for material interests tends to dominate and crowd out the things of the spirit.

Anxiety is disorder. Undue solicitude must be checked and corrected by self-forgetfulness. When we study the conduct of a saint we see that he is concerned primarily about the perfect doing of the heavenly Father's Will. He is deeply interested in the welfare of others, he has comparatively little care for his own. By thus going counter to nature's imperious promptings, he restores the lost balance. He attains harmonious adjustment, perfect sanity, eternal security. In the long run, mankind must adopt this supernatural ideal, must conform to the pattern of life revealed by Jesus. The alternative is chaos first, and then destruction.

Dear Lord, help me to understand the importance of freedom from spiritual anxiety! No one is more perfectly balanced or more imperturbably sane than the disciple who never fears that anything of value will be missed if he maintains harmony of will with God—that ideal relationship between an earthly child and the heavenly Father. If the service of God were to bring no higher reward than perfect peace, it would still be worth the while of any man or woman. "Ah Christ, if there were no hereafter, it still were best to follow Thee!"

After All, These Things the Gentiles Seek (Matt. 6, 32)

L OGICALLY enough, the worldling concentrates attention upon his own affairs. He feels he must depend upon himself. This is in accord with his creed. He has to be self-reliant, because there is no one else upon whom he may rely. His ethical system teaches him to make the most of the present moment—to eat, drink and be merry, since tomorrow he dies.

Surely we do not need to be told how foolish and wrong this sort of behavior would be in the case of a man who has accepted the moral standards set up in the Sermon on the Mount, and who, therefore, knows the divine code by which he is to be judged at the last day. The ideals imposed upon Christ's followers contrast vividly with the aims of the worldling. It would be pos sible to find excuses for a heathen who devoted his life to the seeking of comfort and power and honor; it is not possible to find a valid excuse for this kind of conduct in a Christian. He has committed himself by a public profession to pursue those unworldly aims which have been—at least theoretically—identified with the name of Christ in the pages of the Gospel and in twenty centuries of Christian history.

I cannot even pretend that I am unaware of the obligations imposed upon me by You, dear Lord. All about me I see many disciples who are busily employed in furthering Your cause, by carrying out the Will of the heavenly Father, hour after hour, day after day, year after year. Fathers and mothers and children, missionaries and monks and nuns are devoting time and energy to prayer and good works with amazing indifference to personal comfort and to what the world calls material prospects. When I meditate upon the lesson of these consecrated lives, I can no longer blind myself to the truth that those of us who are concerned primarily with visible, tangible "goods" are not really Christian at heart, but heathen!

Your Father Knows That You Need All These Things
(Matt. 6, 32)

IT WOULD be quite impossible to study the spiritual teaching of Our Lord without becoming aware of His insistence upon the heavenly Father's care for us, His children. It would be equally impossible to observe the characteristics of the saints and yet overlook the quiet serenity with which they commit themselves unafraid to the loving Providence of God. This spirit of trust saturates Our Lord's whole life, all His preaching and all His conduct; it colors His disposition, shapes His behavior, re-echoes in His words; and if, on the Cross, His dying words seem like the despairing cry of outraged nature, they are followed quickly by His last confident commitment of His soul into the hands of His heavenly Father. We cannot remain unmoved at the sight of the martyrs who, in imitation of Him, lay down their lives, joyful, trustful, sure of never being abandoned.

Recognition of absolute dependence on God is an essential element of all real religion. And men are dependent on God not only in the supernatural order of grace, but in the order of nature as well. We must recognize that dependence and all its implications. We must not only remember, but also joyfully accept, our dependence upon the God who is the object of our faith, our hope, our love. Our native helplessness can be quickly driven home to us by illness, by the loss of friends or money, by the disfavor of the mighty, by any set of untoward circumstances.

Dear Lord, shield me from the false and foolish notion of my own sufficiency. Show me the madness of planning even a day of my life without taking into account my dependence upon You. Let me live by faith, by trust, by prayer. I know I am helpless, but for You. I am glad to be dependent on You. And I fear not!

Your Father . . . Maketh His Sun to Rise on the Good and the Evil (Matt. 5, 45)

THIS quiet statement of fact conveys a principle upon which all of us need to meditate. For it reminds us of the even-handed impartiality with which God dispenses His gifts through the laws of nature. The rain and the sun, the heat and the cold, the succession of day and night, the revolution of the seasons, are all without regard to persons. There is no preference or partiality, no distinction. Thinking of this, we reflect how rarely do we find a man who employs a single standard in his dealings with all other men. We hardly expect perfect justice unless we are dealing with saints who are emancipated from subjection to custom and appetite.

If we embody the spirit suggested by the impartial weather and the unprejudiced seasons, we shall embrace within our kinship and affection all the unnumbered millions of our fellow creatures; and we shall extend to them help in the measure made possible by our resources and made desirable by their need. It is no sufficient answer to say that we have obligation. It would not be a sufficient answer to say that we have been injured, or that we have reason to think we may in future be injured by them. One sees at a glance what a different world this would be if the principle just stated were taken seriously as a standard of conduct even by a majority of those who call themselves Christians. For they, at least by implication, subscribe to the belief that all God's children constitute one great family, with the consequent reciprocal duty of extending love and giving aid.

I make my own, dear Lord, the sentiments of that man who prays to be able to fulfill all things which true and perfect justice requires. I hope to extend toward everyone, always, good will, kind words, spiritual and material assistance. May we, all of us, after the example of our heavenly Father, cultivate toward our neighbor a habit of justice and of charity, wide as the sky and deep as the sea.

He Who Seeks, Finds (Matt. 7, 8)

RELUCTANCE to give up what we like is natural to all of us. Self-denial is unpopular. To be sure, most individuals are ready to deny self for the prospect of gain, and all the more ready in proportion as the expected return is large and immediate. This sort of expediency appeals to any normal intelligence on the strictly natural level. In the measure that the expected return becomes less material and more remote, however, the practice of self-denial becomes unfashionable; and this is the case with the Christian virtue of renunciation.

Hence the need to remind ourselves frequently and emphatically that Our Lord offers us what might be described as an incredibly profitable investment. Reluctance to deny self may be more than counterbalanced by a supernatural motive. Once the vision of eternity has captivated a man's imagination, he quickly takes on the characteristics of a hero. St. Paul says, "Eye hath not seen, nor ear heard, neither hath it entered into the heart of man, what things God hath prepared for them that love him."

The crucial test of my power of vision and my strength of will is to be found in my readiness to live and labor, to renounce and suffer, with no sure prospect of any tangible reward during the term of my earthly life. I shall be ready to do these things if I attain to spiritual maturity, and associate myself with the hopes and plans which form the only serious and lasting concern of the saints. Help me, dear Lord, to see things from the viewpoint of death, through Your eyes, in the light of Heaven, through the vista of eternity. Then, and then only, will they be in proper proportion to one another; then, and then only, can I be sure that each choice of mine will be made in conformity with Your Will.

Nor Thieves Break in and Steal (Matt. 6, 20)

THE word "treasure" lends itself easily to Our Lord's use in His lessons on the kingdom of God. There is "good treasure" and "evil treasure." There is "treasure in Heaven," which needs not to be protected against thieves; and treasure on earth, "which the fool layeth up for himself." We are told to remember that where the treasure is, there is the heart also; that the thoughts of worldlings cling to earth, whereas the thoughts of Christians point to Heaven.

Each one of us should have a clear idea of what "treasure" means to us. Commonly the word is applied to material wealth which has to be guarded carefully— money, jewels and the like. But the heavenly treasure to which Our Lord directs attention is something else again. Not moths or rust, nor thieves or devils, can deprive a man of these most precious things, always sufficiently guarded by God's grace and man's good will. There is no cause to wonder when worldly men remain apathetic about their share of the heavenly treasure on which they place no value whatever. But the Christian, if consistent, will make the acquisition of heavenly treasure his chief concern. Otherwise he is like a man of perverted appetite who tries to quench his thirst with sea water, or to satisfy his hunger with food that he knows to be poison.

Dear Lord, I see clearly that I can get nothing worth possessing out of the kind of worldly career which many people regard as eminently desirable. Such a life, unsecured by heavenly treasure, would end as tragic failure. Let me identify myself with Your disciples whose wealth cannot be consumed by moth or rust or carried away by thieves. Though I pass my life as a dish washer and die a public charge, I shall be content if I am numbered among Your faithful followers.

THE authentic saint is gentle. To be sure, he may be also downright vehement, immovable; quite often St. Paul used words that were not mild. Yet gentleness —akin to patience, kindness, meekness—is a property of holiness. By way of proof we need only recall the love and pity and gentleness that were conspicuous in Our Lord's character. If we find a holy man unsympathetic, rude, rough, discourteous, we may safely regard this as one of his "lingering imperfections."

To say the saint is gentle does not mean he is soft. The Roman Emperors—and many another tyrant, ancient and modern—found that out. The saint's will can be as unyielding as a law of nature, when principles are at stake. Nor does being gentle imply being insensitive. The saint who can smile under torture and, like St. Lawrence, jest on the gridiron, has feelings as fine as those of poets and musicians. Note, too, that the gentle saint may not have been born so. He may have progressed toward holiness by learning to control a hot temper and a sharp tongue. The consistently gentle St. Francis de Sales acquired his graciousness after long arduous striving. Once he avoided a meeting with an ill-behaved person for fear of losing the temper which he had labored so long to bring under control. Sometimes fools rush in where saints fear to tread.

Dear Lord, I know I have done harm to others and to myself by harsh judgments, impatience, biting words— by my general lack of gentleness. Help me to be sorry and ashamed. Inspire me to be methodical and diligent in the acquiring of counterhabits which will check my natural meanness. Only if I do this, can I hope to be recognized as kin of Yours, and of Your Mother—Our Blessed Mother, Mary.

Young Man . . . Arise (Luke 7, 14)

AFTER Our Lord had spoken these words, he that was dead sat up. Reading, we may be disposed to ask why are miracles no more; why does Christ not walk abroad in our land today, raising those dead who are very dear to us. The question loses much of its significance, however, when we reflect that we witness miracles far more stupendous. Christ daily gives life or strength to hundreds and thousands of dead or dying souls.

For the spiritual dead and dying lie all about. Sometimes it almost appears as though a law of compensation were exacting payment for material progress; as though vast factories and colossal world markets were crowding out charity and chivalry; as though selfishness were choking aspirations. Greed increases with wealth. As income rises, the hold of religion upon a man, a family, a nation seems to weaken.

You dear Lord, are the Saviour of those ideals for lack of which men's souls will faint and perish. Without Your grace, I am blind to the divine beauty of unselfishness; I do not sufficiently esteem renunciation. Will You, who recalled the widow's son to life, aid me to cast aside the grave clothes of self-indulgence? I know it is idle to beg for Your help, unless I am disposed to make use of it when it comes. So I now promise to examine the habits of self-indulgence which I have been forming; and to commit myself to certain definite decisions. I can make resolutions with regard to speech, for example— both its quantity and its quality. Again my curiosity can be checked!—and should be. And my extravagance! And my temper! I can be more prompt in obeying, less distracted in praying. You have helped me to see—now I must begin to do.

He Is My Brother and Sister and Mother (Mark 3, 35)

FAMILY ties are strong. As the proverb puts it "blood is thicker than water." Not heroes alone, but their kindred as well, receive honor. Tributes paid to greatness are repeated over and over again to descendants. Obligations imposed by family ties extend to generation after generation. Having this in mind, we say "What an honor to be numbered among the kinsfolk of Our Blessed Lord!"

For, as the text reminds us, Jesus considered a blood relationship as nothing when compared with that between Himself and God's faithful servants. You and I then can, as it were, choose the family to which we shall belong, select our own line of descent, establish a relationship recognized as valid in Heaven. We can make ourselves kin to the men and women who have done most for humanity, who deserve best to be imitated. Highest privilege of all, we can make ourselves closer kin of Jesus than those persons who are united to Him by ties of flesh and blood.

Dear Lord, help me to understand the other implications of this principle. For it means that if I turn my back upon You and violate my conscience, I make myself the kinsman of sinners, filthy, revolting, despicable, children of the devil. What I must do, I know, is to repudiate at once the connections which have made me the servant of sin, and then accept Your proffered grace, and thus become as close to You as a brother and sister and mother. Help me to do this, dear Lord, and I will bless You at all times, Your praise shall ever be in my mouth. It is good for me to seek You out, and get close to You, and recognize that You, and You alone, are my hope, my salvation, my glory!

I Have Come to Bring a Sword, Not Peace
(Matt. 10, 34)

AT TIMES the Christian conscience may urge respectful, but firm, resistance to parents, superiors, laws. We are bound to obey God first of all. Political parties have been split and destroyed, educational programs opposed, civil laws disobeyed, business associations broken in the name of conscience and at the bidding of religion. Indeed, traces of blood mark the progress of the Church along the path of history. Fundamental in the Christian code is the principle that the court, parliament, government are subject themselves to a higher law.

Little wonder then if, from time to time, an individual or a whole generation may be called upon to face public disapproval, financial loss, disgrace, violence, death. Experiences such as these have contributed to the welding of a Christian tradition, strong enough to resist successfully all the forces of nature, all human passion, all diabolical ingenuity. I may have to follow conscience at the cost of great suffering and shame. Or my test may come in the doing of comparatively little things day by day; in developing a habit of self-expression sharply different from that which is approved by pagan educators. In fact I realize that the doing of small good deeds that imply discomfort and inconvenience may seem harder than the undertaking of heroic feats.

I understand, dear Lord, that it is You who speak to me when my conscience summons me to the practice of obedience, humility, resignation. When I am true to conscience, I may feel the sharp edge of an unsheathed sword, I may have to endure mortal anguish, but I shall be comforted and peaceful despite my suffering, if the sword has been blessed by Your hands, and if my anguish comes, like Yours in the Garden, from obedience to the Father's Will!

That Your Joy May Be Full (John 16, 24)

THE Christian is not required to exclude joy from his earthly life. Pursuit of holiness is quite compatible with the rational desire to be happy. The one barrier to the wide liberty enjoyed by the children of God is their obligation to accept the standard of value established by Jesus. We may not choose earthly happiness as our final aim, nor exalt pleasure over duty, nor make self the central interest. A bishop who wrote a book on joy affirmed that happiness is an indispensable element of spiritual as of physical health; that "Every man has the need of joy, and the right to joy."

The contrast between the Christian and the pagan concept of happiness is plain enough. It springs from the difference in view about what we commonly call pleasure—the agreeable feeling produced by possession or expectation of a tangible, visible, material "good." The contrast may be symbolized by setting the typical individual accepted by the world as a symbol of joy alongside the typical individual accepted by the Christian—perhaps a millionaire movie star, on the one hand, and on the other a shabbily dressed saint. We must not assume that the former has solid grounds for joy. We may be quite sure that the latter has.

I have often heard that happiness and holiness go together. I recall St. Philip Neri's declaration that the servant of God must always be good humored. I remember the old monk's words that a good conscience is joyful even amid adversities, whereas an evil conscience is fearful and restless always. Once again, dear Lord, I take to heart the lesson that You will remain the source of my joy although all others should foresake me. Once again I remind myself that if I am loyal to You, I shall surely be happy; but if I separate from You, I shall do myself more harm than the whole world and all my enemies could ever do.

Did You Lack Anything? (Luke 22, 35)

SOMETIMES a subtle reproach is more effective than a weapon. This is especially true when the reproach is intended to stimulate a resolution of amendment. It is most notably true, when the reproach is directed toward a person of fine instincts—one who will be hurt deeply by the consciousness of having failed to meet the expectations of friendship or the demands of duty.

There is no need for me to ask if Our Lord's words to the Apostles apply also to me. The answer is obvious. They do. He has been magnificently generous. I should therefore ask: "Why do I not make adequate return to Our Lord for His gifts to me?" To that the answer is, because I spend too much time and devote too much attention to myself—to my comfort, food, relaxation, fine clothing. Forgetting Our Lord's lessons, I neglect to follow the rule He laid down for His disciples—to leave everything in His hands. I concern myself with possible ways of winning the first seat and the center of the stage. In one word, I am always busily engaged with my past, present and future interests.

Let me come to grips with reality. Let me not shrink from facing the truths You taught, dear Lord. Let me study the picture that You have drawn. It makes plain the serious consequences of wilful delay, of stubborn blindness, of that forgetfulness which is equivalent to disobedience. If I fail to keep my eyes open when I am on the brink of danger, I cannot be excused from fault. If I do keep them open, I shall hardly act as if I were unaware of the shortness of life, the approach of death, the eternity of judgment; and I shall have the unspeakable bliss of being welcomed to Heaven as Your faithful servant and friend.

Do You Not Remember? (Mark 8, 18)

WHATEVER point of view we take, we easily see the vital part that memory plays in life. It is a determining factor in critical issues, on every level—physical, mental, religious. Memory—according as it is strong or weak—will make or break a man in his effort to secure an education, to get a better job, to win or retain the respect and affection of others, to avoid misfortunes, to profit by opportunities in the field of health, of economic security, of social popularity. Our Lord's words make plain that in our dealing with Him it is sometimes sinful to "forget." This is a matter that deserves careful consideration.

When we ask why it is sinful to forget, we find that the question answers itself. We cannot escape blame, if we handle precious things carelessly, if we regard solemn warnings lightly, if we look at divine truths drowsily and inattentively. Habitual irreverence and disrespect play a large part in our failure to keep in touch with God and to become increasingly sensitive to His influence. And all this happens because we do not train ourselves to adjust our conduct strictly to the spiritual standards established by Our Lord. Merely because there is no prospect of quick punishment, no master near us with a whip, we take advantage of the situation, forgetting that this is shutting our eyes to the light.

Dear Lord, may I faithfully use the light that You have given me, so that I may deserve to be numbered among the children of the light. I shrink from the thought that my forgetfulness is really a symptom of an unloving heart; and yet I cannot but recognize the contrast between my careless, negligent conduct and the loyal attention to Your words and wishes which is characteristic of Your true friends. The prayer I make now is that You will help me, so that in the future I may remember.

16th WEEK AFTER PENTECOST—SUNDAY
The Sabbath Was Made for Man (Mark 2, 27)

THESE words shamed the Pharisees. Exact and literal in conforming to the Mosaic law in order that they might be considered faithful Jews, they were at heart indifferent to the glory of God and the welfare of their neighbors. They forgot the essentials of religion; they thought much of small details. Our Lord recalled them to basic principles—as He often did: "It is the spirit that gives life, the flesh is of no avail"; "The inner is more important than the outer"; "Man is better than a sheep"; "First things come first, not last." He keeps ever reminding us that, when a human will fits into the divinely established order, God's likeness is developed; when we ignore the divine order by substituting self for God, the keystone is destroyed and the whole arch comes tumbling down.

At the basis of Christian philosophy of life is the undying conviction that no soul may ever be used as a means to an end. Reverence for human personality must dominate every field of activity—domestic, social, political, religious. Human rights are inviolable. Even the Sabbath was made for man, for his moral welfare and spiritual development, his growth into godlikeness.

When You, dear Lord, looked around at the Pharisees, You were "grieved at the blindness of their hearts." How often You must be grieved at mine. There are souls that have become less holy or less happy because of me. I have harmed them by temper, by injustice. I have by word or deed led them to think that wrong is right, or that a great sin is only a little sin. Often I have had a share—be it never so small—in the success of a bad book, or an evil entertainment. For all sins of this kind, I now beg pardon.

16th WEEK AFTER PENTECOST—MONDAY
The Father Himself Loves You (John 16, 27)

WITHIN our nature we sense at times a deep hunger for friendship. Whatever his pose, whatever his boast, no normal man is happy if utterly alone. Not even God Himself is a single Person. And in every human heart, there is, whether recognized or not, a deep need for affection. Because no relationship between creatures can be wholly satisfying, and because none can possibly be lasting, the perfect satisfaction of man's longing for companionship must be found in God.

That hunger for a perfect, yet unattainable friendship, therefore, is like the stirring of a deep instinct which points to God as the one final goal of all our striving. It is like the echo of the ancient voice which cried out, "Thou hast made us for Thyself, Oh God, and our soul is restless until it finds rest in Thee." A penetrating study of the human heart led a theologian to write: "God is the anonymous object of every desire." For God alone can effectively quench the thirst of the soul for beauty and truth and holiness.

Too late have I known You, O heavenly Father! Too late have I loved You. No longer will I grieve You. No more will I be cold and indifferent. Let me never again forget You. Let me never be deaf to Your speaking. I will watch You as a servant watches his Master to learn Your Will. I will make it my joy to please You in everything. Hold me back from the call of pleasure, of friends, of self. Help me to face fearlessly the threat of pain. Be You my guide, my leader always—the one and only object of my worship. Speak, Lord, Your servant heareth. Help me to heed. Behold the servant of the Lord!

16th WEEK AFTER PENTECOST—TUESDAY
The Things That Are to Come, He Will Declare to You
(John 16, 13)

PROVERBIALLY it is easier to preach than to practice. With regard to issues which do not affect us personally, we are judicial, detached; we consider them calmly; we give an impartial verdict. One charts dispassionately enough the shoals and quicksands of a perilous sea upon which one does not have to sail. It is quite another story when we turn from theory to action. Then we are like the man in the fable who, having saved many others by wise advice, could not keep out of trouble himself.

The phrase "wishful thinking" reflects a common tendency. Consciously or unconsciously, I tend to believe that whatever promises pleasure or profit is really true, that my heart's desire will eventually be gratified. As soon as personal interests are involved, new considerations come to stimulate emotion, to color judgment, to sway the will. Things fall out of focus in my mind. Proportions are distorted. Hopes and wishes lead me astray from the trail of truth. Only one type of wishful thinking can guide a man infallibly—the desire to see God's Will accomplished. This is a true compass; I may set my course safely by it. For, at long last, God's Will is always done.

The gift of counsel, which counterbalances the pressure of selfish emotion, will enable me to see things as they really are. It does much more. It lifts me up to a higher level, gives my vision a wider range, plays the light of faith upon objects infinitely distant, bestows on me the power to look into eternity. May I make good use of this gift! May I be much more alert to follow wise advice than to attempt to give it. To my soul may the faintest whisper of the Holy Spirit be always divinely true, divinely convincing. Whatever He suggests is to be carried out at once—"no sooner said than done." I will never disregard counsel which it would be moral insanity, spiritual suicide, to neglect.

Seek, and You Shall Find (Matt. 7, 7)

THERE is a natural correspondence between the seeker and the thing sought. Observing the dominant, primary interests of a young person, one may—if sufficient opportunity be given—predict the profession or vocation that should be chosen, and the probable chances of success. Heads of novitiates, officials in charge of guidance, learn much about an aspirant by noting the aspirant's desires. Tell me what a person is ever thinking about, looking for, spending time and energy on; and I can tell you whether he is wise or foolish, reasonable or sensual.

It should not be very difficult to distinguish between nominal Christians and wholehearted Christians. We need only take note of the aims which they pursue: Does this professed disciple greatly love money and the things that money can buy? Is he more concerned to get rid of his faults, or to make a good impression upon other men? Does he devote much or little time to prayer? Is he as greatly distressed at finding that he has neglected the poor as he is at receiving a social slight? Our Lord has pointed out the sure road on which we must travel, if we are ever to gain the greatest good. He gives us a star by which to steer.

In so many ways, dear Lord, and on so many occasions, You have tried to correct my defective vision, to make me see clearly the difference between what is genuine and what is spurious. And I still give much time and thought to things not worth the seeking. Once again I beg of You the great gift of heavenly light; once again I pray that, with the aid of the Holy Spirit, I may relish the things that are right, and ever rejoice in His consolation.

16th WEEK AFTER PENTECOST—THURSDAY
He Who Loses His Life for My Sake, Will Find It
(Matt. 10, 39)

ALTHOUGH the qualities of strength, courage, zeal, moral independence, are praised highly in the Gospels, the virtue of "fortitude" is not named. It does occur in the Acts of the Apostles where the first martyr, St. Stephen, is called "a man full of faith and of the Holy Spirit . . . full of grace and power." The Church recognizes fortitude as a cardinal virtue and as one of the gifts of the Holy Ghost.

In few respects has the influence of grace been more visibly potent than in the transformation of weak and timid into strong, courageous souls. A sort of standing miracle makes children, women and peaceful unarmed men, brave enough to defy and resolute enough to overcome the whole world. Out of unsuspected depths the disciples of Jesus have time and again brought forth a fortitude literally irresistible. To be sure, pagan philosophers also have stood against brute force, "bloody but unbowed"; and war has its heroes, too. But Christian fortitude, simple, humble, confessedly a gift of God, has a distinctive quality all its own. A St. Agnes, a St. Cecilia, a St. Lawrence, leave the pagan world troubled and mystified by their indifference to shame and their cheerful endurance of torment. The claim of the disciple is literally true, "I can do all things in Him who strengthens me."

It is not only in the torture room, not only in times of savage persecution, that our souls need to be strengthened by the indwelling Spirit of God. Many a hidden slave of duty, many a patient victim of endless temptation, many an ordinary Christian who would repudiate all claim to heroism, stand out in the sight of edified observers as living proofs of the strength that comes out of weakness when the designs of God are not resisted. To be numbered among these is the vocation of the average Christian. Dear Lord, help all of us—help me especially—to fulfill it.

I Send You . . . Wise Men and Scribes (Matt. 23, 34)

HUMAN beings tend to forget that even their noblest aspirations need not be adjusted by an external standard. Alone, we explore vast realms of thought, speculating on human problems; but, from time to time, we must come down from the lonely height, or the ivory tower; we must emerge from our secret laboratory or private study, in order to correct private findings and personal conclusions by checking them against the thoughts and observations of fellow mortals. Many a fanatic, many a false mystic went fantastically astray because he lived in an imaginary universe created by himself.

No wonder then, that Christ provided for man's need of contact with other men in matters of faith. Not as solitaries, do we learn what we must believe and what we should do. Jesus who came to show us the path to Heaven, who revealed many enlightening truths about the heavenly Father, who told us plainly how to behave in order to please God, also bade us keep in touch with our fellowmen. In order to be safe from illusion, we must have the help of others. We must learn from those whom God has appointed to teach and to lead.

I am thankful, dear Lord, that You have saved me from the danger of going astray by providing me with a check, a test. This safeguard, I know, is far more necessary in religion than in other fields. I will try to be responsive to whatever You say to me through those whom You have appointed to guide me. I think with humble gratitude of the blessed privilege I enjoy of being enlightened and inspired by Your Church, Your priests, Your saints, canonized and uncanonized. Often by speech, sometimes by conduct, sometimes merely by reputation, I have been given precisely the help I needed. For this blessing may I be always profoundly thankful!

He Who Hears You Hears Me (Luke 10, 16)

MUCH IS written and said today about the reconciling of faith and science, revelation and reason. At times, in consequence, men lose sight of the essentially supernatural character of Christianity. To be sure, there is a correspondence between the truths of religion and our natural aspirations. Faith solves problems and allays cravings that would otherwise torment the soul; science, philosophy, logic give support to various articles of the Christian creed. Yet we must always remember that authority, not argument, provides the real basis of faith. The rights of reason remain inviolate; Our Lord taught nothing that is self-contradictory. But He did teach truths that unaided reason could never attain, and also truths that reason, at its best, can never comprehend.

Our religion, then, is a religion of authority. In the last analysis we believe truths because God has conveyed them to us through the Church which He established for this precise purpose. We hold to the articles of the Creed, not because we can prove them to ourselves or to others, but because they have come from a divine Teacher. With her finger on the pulse of humanity, the Church accompanies us in our progress, ministering to our needs, helping us in our struggles, whispering to us of God. She is thus preparing every sinful man for the moment when, tired of puzzles and deceits, he will turn to Christ.

I believe in You, God the Father Almighty, Maker of Heaven and earth, and of all things visible and invisible. I believe in You, Lord Jesus Christ, only-begotten Son of God; born of the Father before all ages; God of God, Light of Light; true God of true God. I believe in the Holy Spirit, the Lord and Giver of life, who proceedeth from the Father and Son. I believe in one, holy, Catholic, and apostolic Church. And for the gift of faith I thank You, dear Lord and Master!

Thou Shalt Love the Lord Thy God. . . . This Is the Greatest and the First Commandment (Matt. 22, 37-38)

NOTHING can equal, nothing can be substituted for, the love of God. Whatever develops and deepens this love is good—and is good on that account. So also whatever interferes with or weakens it is bad—and just for that reason. In this twofold principle, we find a practical measure of the value of thought, word and deed. Thus we may discover if we are heading toward Heaven or toward hell.

If we have had sound religious training, we know the truth just stated. Elementary faith impresses upon us the absolute worth of God. Nothing can even exist unless through dependence upon Him; from Him all else obtains whatever value it may possess. To turn away from Him and seek a different "good" is to stultify ourselves, to betray our own intelligence. A creature cannot rationally and consistently prefer any other object or person to Him. One who understands the nature of love knows that only by loving God first are we able to love truly at all.

Over and over again, dear Lord, You have made it clear that my chief aim in life must be to keep aware of Your Presence and to conform my will perfectly to Yours. At times the whole universe, every person and all things, seem to be in a conspiracy to blind me, or dazzle me, or at least to make me forgetful. But my only prospect of attaining the joy which You have prepared for me depends upon my giving You the first place in my thought and my affection. Grant me, O Lord, the grace that will enable me to avoid the enticements of the evil spirit so that with a pure mind and a brave heart I may follow wherever You lead!

Woe to You . . . Because You . . . Disregard . . . the Love of God (Luke 11, 42)

CHARITY, greatest of the fundamental virtues, is the simplest. It is also the most necessary. Moreover, it is within the reach of everyone. The exercise of charity is in order every day and almost every hour, in each home, in each place of work. It does not consist chiefly in giving away money. It manifests itself most of all in sympathy, in patience, in unselfish affection. To be kind and gentle and loving is as much above the offering of material gifts as the soul is superior to the body, as Heaven is above earth.

Charity is not only a necessary condition of being a Christian; it is also the fulfilling of the law. In one who is really perfect in charity there can be nothing wanting. With such a one God will be well pleased. This is, after all, the best possible inducement to strive to acquire charity. To have gained it at much cost and after many years of striving, will be a guarantee of Heaven. What can keep us from attempting a work however hard, when to its accomplishment so great a reward is attached?

It might be a good thing every morning when saying my prayers to repeat St. Paul's words: "Without charity I am nothing"—and then to reflect for a moment upon the temptations to violate charity which will probably confront me in the course of the day. Dear Lord, teach me to be kind to all, even my enemies; keen-sighted and alert to help others; deaf when rude words are spoken; forgiving when my patience is tried; ready to relinquish good things; content with the lowest place. Then will life be fairer and happier to me and to all with whom I come in contact; and I shall be daily brought nearer and nearer to the kingdom of God.

What Do You Think of the Christ? Whose Son Is He?
(Matt. 22, 42)

To THE question addressed by Our Lord to the Pharisees, the correct answer could be found in the words of the heavenly Father "This is my beloved Son." As God, Jesus is the Son of the heavenly Father; as Man, He is the son of Our Lady, the Blessed Virgin Mary. Remembering this, we think again of those who, despite their reverence for Our Lord and His Father, seem to cherish a sort of dislike, or fear, of His Mother —as if it were possible for even the greatest of creatures to trespass upon the rights of God.

We recall the loving memories that were stamped upon the heart of our Blessed Lady, most perfect of merely human beings and closest to her divine Son—images that no other creature was ever privileged to possess. All her life long she dwelt upon the days and months and years that had passed since the first Christmas night in Bethlehem—upon scenes and words intertwined with her worship of the omnipotent Lord of Heaven and earth who had created her. These memories formed the ever expanding background of her consciousness as she saw Jesus growing up by her side, going forth on His mission to teach and to save, living out the last tragic days of His earthly life.

Dear Lord, I believe that You were conceived of the Holy Spirit and born of the Virgin Mary, who is blessed above all women and is so called by all generations. Help me to commune with Your Mother, whom You have shared with us, as not merely an ideal, but a real being. Remote as we reckon years, she is still always living. Help me to be truly her child. Fix in my mind a sense of the vital personal relationship that binds her to me; and help me to behave in a way that will please her!

17th WEEK AFTER PENTECOST—WEDNESDAY
How Is It That You Sought Me? (Luke 2, 49)

THESE are the first words that the Gospel records as having been spoken by Jesus to His Mother. The question is of the type called "rhetorical"; it requires no answer. A mother's love easily overflows into anxiety. To Mary, when her Son was absent, the world seemed empty. This would be true of almost any mother; it was especially true of her. Strange, indeed, had she not "sought Jesus sorrowing."

When we meditate upon the relationship between Our Lord and His Mother, we are reminded of the relationship which should exist between Him and ourselves. We are moved now to think that a question which Jesus might fittingly address to us would be: "How is it that you have *not* sought Me?" For few of us are sufficiently concerned about seeking Him, living in His Presence, maintaining with Him a constant harmony of wills. Many legends and anecdotes illustrate the fact that holy men and women have the habit of keeping their minds fixed on the divine Presence amid all sort of occupations and despite all sorts of distractions. To seek Him and to abide with Him is their chief concern.

"O dearest Saviour, Thou soughtest me when I fled from Thee! Wilt Thou reject me now that I seek Thee?" I know, dear Lord, I do not seek You as diligently as I should. I am not as mindful of Your Presence as I might be. Let me resolve that henceforward—this day and every day—I will frequently enter into that inner solitude from which all creatures are excluded, and there, for a little while at least, abide with You. Even though I am called upon to mingle with other persons and to perform distracting duties, I will not overlook my opportunity to commune with You, to speak and then in turn to listen, as lover and beloved ever do!

17th WEEK AFTER PENTECOST—THURSDAY
Have I Not a Right to Do What I Choose?
(Matt. 20, 15)

THE distribution of God's gifts presents an insoluble puzzle. We cannot understand why He gives apparently so much to one and apparently so little to another. This problem holds good for natural gifts as well as for grace. We wonder why God is not moved, as we are moved by pity, to eliminate sordid poverty. We would heal all the crippled and all the blind; we would quickly relieve agonizing pain; we would shower about a profusion of such blessings as strength of character and spiritual vision. If we had the power to arrange it so, men would have more faith and more hope; and victory over temptation would be much easier, much more common. At least, so we think.

Although we cannot explain God's dispensation of graces, this proves nothing against His wisdom and goodness. It is merely one more problem of the many to which human wisdom finds no perfectly satisfactory solution. But so surely as God is God, no man is ever forgotten, or ever badly treated. Our heavenly Father may be safely trusted to maintain justice. He will set all things in order—if not visibly, here and now, then at some other time and place, or else at long last in eternity.

Dear Lord, I am more certain of Your goodness than of my own intelligence. I have wholehearted, all-inclusive trust in You. I know that everyone who suffers patiently for Your sake, will receive splendid recognition, a rich reward. All the days of my life—especially in those days when I am disturbed at the sight of others who lack blessings that have been given me, persons who suffer pain or disgrace or any other kind of hardship— I will retain blind unquestioning confidence in Your goodness. What is not clear to me by reason, I see by faith. I know that Your ways are not our ways indeed; yet they are right, always right, perfectly right, divinely right!

17th WEEK AFTER PENTECOST—FRIDAY

It Is . . . the Spirit of Your Father Who Speaks Through You (Matt. 10, 20)

OUR generation stresses the value of independence. Unfortunately, however, some persons entertain the absurd notion that they are independent even of God. Indeed, there are some who go so far as to affirm that human co-operation makes God richer, stronger, and able to do what otherwise He could not do. This is to exaggerate the human at the expense of the divine. God, being infinite, has unlimited power. Nothing lies outside the range of omnipotence. We are dust, or sand, or less than these, when compared with God.

One of the first lessons in spiritual wisdom is that our highest possible development means growth in likeness to God. Only in the measure that we reproduce His ideas, or achieve something like a copy of His work, shall we attain to full stature, achieve a masterpiece. To belittle the divine and exaggerate the human is a dragging down, not an exalting, of our standards. The path of progress is blocked when men substitute the finite for the infinite, the material for the spiritual, the trivial for the sublime. This is anthropomorphism at its worst; it is in sharp contrast with St. Paul's appeal to imitate Christ, so majestic in personality, so world-stirring in influence.

Dear Lord, save me from being led away by the false wisdom which craftily uses my egotism and plays upon my pride. I know well that only by unconditional surrender to Your grace can I reach any goal worth my striving. It was in the following of You that the most heroic characters in history found their development and splendidly served their fellowmen. It was by this means that the foolish overcame the wise and the weak became strong. Help us all to heed the warning against being wise in our own conceits!

Out of the Abundance of the Heart the Mouth Speaks
(Matt. 12, 34)

THOSE who study the teaching of the saints are used to admonitions on the value of silence. It comes to them as a surprising discovery that silence is mentioned so seldom in the Gospels, whereas by contrast we come upon frequent recommendations with regard to speech. The words of Our Lord quoted above remind us that Christians spontaneously, almost irresistibly, speak about things that rank as most precious in their judgment. Whereas gossip, malicious criticism, wasteful and idle words are rigorously excluded, speech for the sake of recreation and friendly talks about common interests have a share in ordinary conversation.

Although silence has its place then, we may, indeed we must, sometimes speak. Not even the Trappist or Carthusian foregoes entirely the use of his tongue, or wholly ceases to convey his thoughts and resolutions to other men by the use of articulate speech. But it would not be too lofty an aspiration for us to hope that no one would ever suffer the least harm from listening to us.

In the light of these considerations, I see how much there is to correct in my habits of speech. On certain topics I should never touch at all; on others I should dwell briefly and carefully; I should employ my speech as an instrument of good. Let me think now not only of the evil I may have done, but also of the good that I have left undone—of the empty intervals that might have been filled with kind and encouraging words, of the persons who would have greatly profited by information which I could easily have given.

18th WEEK AFTER PENTECOST—SUNDAY
Who . . . Is a Faithful and Prudent Servant?
(Matt. 24, 45)

THE faithful servant is the man who keeps God's word. That is to say, he is the man who conforms to the divine Will as formulated in the Commandments and the Church's precepts, in the directions of superiors, in the bidding of conscience. Some of these obligations concern big things; some of them concern matters in themselves quite insignificant. Some of them are hard to observe; some are very easy. But there they are— the very wishes of God; and we shall never find any other means of attaining happiness than in the fulfilling of them.

How faithfully am I conforming to the word of God? It speaks to me of charity, of honesty, of purity, of prayer. How far may I be regarded as an example of these virtues. Day after day, hour after hour, new opportunities come to me. I meet people who seem to be selfish, unkind, impatient, ill-tempered, unfair, unreasonable. But each time they display these traits they give me an opportunity to exercise patience and gentleness— an opportunity to heed God's word. If I heed it not, then I shall have missed one more opportunity of pleasing Him. If I do heed it, I shall be blessed; and happy will they be who dwell in the same house with me.

Today, not once but probably many times, I shall come upon a chance to prove my fidelity. Shall I, or shall I not accept disappointment graciously, smilingly? Shall I avoid annoyance or embarrassment by telling an untruth, or shall I not? Dear Lord, let me be a faithful servant. Let me realize that the chance of my life is not to come on a far off, distant day, not up in the clouds; it is here, it is now. If I make the most of my opportunities, I shall be blessed beyond the wildest human dreams of happiness!

You Must Be Born Again (John 3, 7)

SPIRITUAL rebirth, as Our Lord explained to Nicodemus, does not mean that the disciple must enter again into his mother's womb, or be wrapped in swaddling clothes, or be laid in a cradle. One has to become a child in reverence, in affection, in obedience. Other qualities and tendencies which are less admirable, we do not acquire. A cynical child would be odious; a cruel child is a monster. No true disciple of Christ can be like that.

When St. Paul became a man, he put away childish things. He did, however, retain childlike simplicity, docility, affection, enthusiasm. The Holy Spirit fosters those qualities within us. His gift of piety not only suggests, but also helps to produce a habit of mind and conduct uncalculating, generous to the point of recklessness, never self-sufficient, always eager to be taught. Because of our relationship with the heavenly Father, piety makes us one great family; it forms us into loving brothers and sisters. The family home, which is truly God's house, may be recognized by the likeness of its atmosphere to that of Nazareth.

The kindness which is inseparable from patience, the unfailing courtesy which requires constant self-denial, the sympathetic consideration which is the antithesis of egotism, the trustfulness which excludes envy and suspicion—these make up the piety which will reign in every household where the influence of the Holy Spirit is unopposed. These indicate the qualities which I should possess; and which, if I do not possess, I should labor diligently to acquire. My mirror reflects the face of one who falls far short of the moral beauty, symmetry, that are characteristic traits of Christ. I find myself ugly, misshapen. And this, I realize, is my own fault. God helping me, I am going to become less unlike what I should be!

You Therefore Have Sorrow Now (John 16, 22)

THERE is a kind of sorrow which does not discredit us either in the sight of God or in the eyes of men. A Christian is not supposed to be gay, or indifferent, in the presence of brokenhearted victims of misfortune. On the contrary, to a certain extent he suffers with them—as the very meaning of the word "sympathy" implies. To be aloof, cold-hearted, untouched by the pain or grief of others, is to be less than human, not more.

Yet it does happen, at times, that the answer to the question: "Why am I sorrowful?" will uncover a motive which does me no honor. I may be sad because I am paying too much attention to depressing facts in my own immediate environment. The disciples on the road to Emmaus, for example, were looking at one part of the picture only. True, Christ had died; but either they had forgotten His promise to rise again, or they were doubtful of His ability to make that promise good. Selfish sorrow often results from our taking a short range, not a long range, view. We need a better sense of proportion. If we face all reality, if we take into account everything both far and near, Heaven as well as earth, eternity no less than time, we shall not be overcome with selfish sorrow.

I have Your assurance, dear Lord, that all things work together for good, if I but love You. When I give this truth the importance it deserves, I am armed against the slings and arrows. Help me to turn the clouds in my sky about and see their silver lining. Help me also to endure my own discomforts, so that I may be able to bring consolation to others. Thus I shall give my neighbors a better opinion of religion; and I shall be a little less unlike the saints.

Do Not Let Your Heart Be Troubled, or Be Afraid
(John 14, 27)

O^N THE subject of fear the teaching of Jesus is in striking contrast with that of the world. The fear of God is excluded from the pagan's pattern of living. Worldlings encourage fear of whatever threatens life, liberty and the pursuit of happiness; they concern themselves with the evils of tyranny, of want, of illness, of insecurity. But as for the danger of offending God— the only danger to which saints are acutely sensitive— this does not disturb the world. Jesus, on the contrary, bids us fear to offend God. That is the ultimate evil; that is the one risk never to be taken for any motive or in any circumstances.

Worldly courage is largely bravado, or ignorance, or forgetfulness. The sinner who fears not God is akin to the maniac who swallows carbolic acid or jumps into a fire. Fear of the Lord is the beginning of wisdom. Among the gifts of the Holy Spirit is fear. St. Augustine, who has much to say on this subject, teaches that the soul, in its progress toward holiness, will gradually eliminate fears; but that it still can be really frightened at the prospect of offending God. This pure fear, *timor castus,* is a holy sentiment. It is free from selfish alloy. It makes for union with God. It helps to develop courage, trust, serenity, peace.

Many of us—far too many—are not as much afraid of offending God as we are disturbed, even alarmed, over those things which worldlings fear. Here we have another example of the way in which the views of Christians diverge from the opinions of the world. Dear Lord, I see that it would be enlightening were I to make an inventory of my fears. I could thus learn whether my design for living bears a closer resemblance to Your plan than to the world's.

I Will Give You Rest (Matt. 11, 28)

To MANY persons—especially to irreligious persons—it seems amazing that the poor, the sick, the crippled, can be gay. Gay they often are, notably the blind —possibly because the blind can most easily exclude distractions and focus their inner vision upon consoling things. The reason why we others are relatively helpless under the blows of misfortune may be that we have made ourselves too dependent upon pleasant experiences and congenial surroundings—in this respect not greatly unlike the drug addict.

Freest of all souls and most truly joyful is the saint, who depends upon no other thing than God—and God he is always conscious of possessing. The price of what we may call the higher gaiety is detachment from the lower. If at times the price—that is to say, detachment from creatures—seems high, we must remember that it is really but a small price, when compared with what is gained. For God's gift of Himself to the soul implies that the soul's capacity for joy is filled, that the saturation point has been reached, that this high degree of bliss will be unending.

In some mysterious way the soul that has God is ensured against the loss of anything worth having. I cannot understand this mystery; for it involves the relationship of the finite to the infinite, of the temporal to the eternal; but I do believe that when I renounce and sacrifice other things for the sake of God, I cannot in any sense be a loser. I stand to gain, inevitably—even though no one can imagine how. Help me, dear Lord, to be completely and exclusively dependent upon You for my prospects of some day possessing all that I really long for.

You Search the Scriptures (John 5, 39)

THIS text is a reminder that few of us read the Bible frequently and attentively as we should—although the Church urgently recommends the habit of Scripture reading. Sometimes we find that non-Catholics are far more zealous than ourselves in the study of the Scriptures. We are even put to shame by unbelieving scholars who devote themselves to the study of ancient manuscripts in order to deepen their knowledge of the Bible.

What a great gift it is, this collection of books written by divine inspiration. It tells us of the relationship between God and man all through history, looking back to Eden and forward to the last judgment. It describes the first disobedience which "brought death into the world and all our woe"; it records the promise of a Messiah; and in stories that have been stamped indelibly on the imagination of mankind, it outlines the slow development of the people of Israel under the Old Testament. The New Testament narrates Gabriel's visit to the Blessed Virgin, the life of Christ as child, as youth, as prophet, the story of the Last Supper and the Passion. Then comes the conversion of St. Paul, his journeys and his writings, and the beginnings of Church history.

In a memorable passage the *Imitation of Christ* speaks of the Body of Christ and the Scripture as necessary to the faithful soul. To You, dear Lord, my thanks for these two tables—the holy altar which bears Your precious Body and the table of the divine law which contains Your holy doctrine. Help me to achieve due reverence and affection for the Sacred Body which You provide for my spiritual nourishment and for the sacred Word which You have set as a lamp unto my feet.

You Know Not the Scriptures (Matt. 22. 29)

N<small>O ONE</small> familiar with the saints can be unaware of their love for the Sacred Writings. The Divine Office contains homilies and commentaries that reflect the meditations of holy persons through long ages of Christian history. Religious communities include Scripture reading among prescribed spiritual exercises. Every man in major holy orders is obliged to recite daily a considerable portion of the sacred text; and the Church encourages all her children to read the Scriptures by the promise of a definite spiritual reward in the form of an indulgence.

Sometimes—the Second Epistle of St. Peter warns—"the unlearned and the unstable distort . . . the Scriptures"; and radical divergence of belief is inevitable when the interpreting of the Bible text is left to private judgment. Acting as divinely commissioned interpreter, the Church makes plain to us the true significance of the Incarnation; the real meaning of "This is My Body"; the power entrusted to the Apostles and their successors; the means provided by Christ for the forgiveness of sin; the relationship between God's grace and man's free will; the nature and sanctity of marriage; the inalienable rights of the individual and the divine limitations of state authority; and the judgment which the soul must face after death.

I see, as every normal human being must see, that I need someone to aid me in the interpretation of the Sacred Writings, so helpful and enlightening if they are properly used, and so easily turned into a source of error otherwise. Thinking of the way in which You have anticipated my need, I am again moved to gratitude for Your great goodness to us, dear Lord.

A King . . . Made a Marriage Feast for His Son
(Matt. 22, 2)

To COMMENTATORS, the marriage feast of the king's son suggests the wedding of the divine and the human natures of Our Lord—that mysterious, consoling truth on which we cannot meditate too often. It was the purpose of the Incarnation to bring God and man together. Splendidly was that purpose fulfilled. Christ dwelt here visibly; He grew and labored; He spoke and suffered and died. A man among men, He was also God among men. With His coming, new cords of strength and patience and holiness were twisted inextricably into the fibers of the human heart. God, closer than ever before, was stamped upon the imagination of the race—an ineffaceable image of perfection.

Christian history shows the blending of God's thoughts and actions with those of men down through the centuries. Our Lord never abandoned the race He came to save at any price; He has been with us in every time and place; He is with us here and now. For all its gloom and shadow and streaks of blood, for all its blindness, hardness and leaden-footed following of heroic leadership—Christian civilization displays the ever present influence of a divine ideal.

Echoing the prayer of the old Carthusian of Coutances, I give You thanks O Lord, Jesus Christ, most perfect God and Man, and most faithful Lover, for the unmeasured charity which caused You to unite our human nature to Yourself, and while remaining perfect God to become perfect Man, to suffer and die! I desire to remain ever in Your sight. I revere Your Presence. I acknowledge Your wisdom, goodness and power. I put my trust in Your infinite and eternal love. I think of You and I worship You with my whole mind and heart!

Father . . . Glorify Thy Son (John 17, 1)

THE liturgy serves to measure the Church's gratitude for the Eucharist. In her expression of thankfulness, she exhausts her resources. Light, flowers, incense, music, poetry, solemn procession, public prayer, make up a liturgical pageantry, splendid, universal, everlasting —a unique phenomenon in the history of the human race. What else could have been done beyond what the Church has so lovingly and constantly done to publish appreciation of the gift made to her on the first Holy Thursday!

In addition to the external, official response of grateful Christendom, we have the inner, private, humble, response of individuals—in no sense less precious to God. In ways innumerable, men give back to Christ their heart's best. The wise men from the East brought the Infant Saviour no gift as precious as those which have been offered on countless occasions by men and women whose hands were empty of earthly wealth. From these Our Lord has received what most of all He sought, the soul's offering of itself. They visit the Blessed Sacrament by day; they keep the vigil by night. One finds them in the majestic cathedral, the country church, the little oratory. Memorable to them is the day of their First Communion. Of supreme importance is their last. Some of those who worship possess untainted, angelic innocence; others have been recently cleansed from iniquity by sorrow and sacramental grace. In every sort of place, from every sort of person, Jesus in the Sacrament of the Altar receives the best men have to give.

Let me then offer thanks for the gift of the Eucharist, both in public and in private. Let me, in all circumstances, take great joy in making reverent acknowledgment of God's goodness. When I join in the wisely planned, deeply impressive liturgy of the Church, and when I offer up my private prayer, I will try, dear Lord, to give You the best I have—to give my all!

I and the Father Are One (John 10, 30)

ST. JOHN is called the beloved disciple because he was admitted to the closest intimacy with Our Lord. There is a certain significance in the fact that, in comparison with the other Evangelists, he affirms Our Lord's divinity more emphatically and more repeatedly. The opening words of his Gospel deal with the eternal life of the Word of God who, in the course of time, "was made Flesh, and dwelt among us." It was upon the consciousness of the friend to whom He was nearest of all, that Our Lord's divinity was thus deeply impressed.

There is a lesson for us here. Sometimes we ask why our old fervor has faded away. Or we may wonder about the reason why such and such a person has given up the faith. Or we may speculate on the motives for the amazing slowness of another who for so long a time has seemed to be on the point of becoming a convert. In all three cases the answer to the problem may perhaps be found in the general principle that the soul nearest to Our Lord is the one that believes in Him most readily, most completely, most loyally. We may well ask for a special grace which will enable us to see more clearly, as life goes on, the deep meaning of the truth upon which St. John consistently dwells.

I know that, from the beginning of my existence, the heavenly Father has been enlightening me; and I know that I have made too little use of that divine illumination. Make increasingly plain to me, dear Lord, that my deep desire to be filled with God can indeed be satisfied, if and when my soul approaches You—You, who have lived among us in the form of flesh and blood. You wish to live over again in the soul of each disciple. You wish to bestow upon each one of us that Gift of Yourself which will make us inexpressibly, eternally happy! I wish to receive it—and to receive it often.

Before Abraham Came to Be, I Am (John 8, 58)

WEIGHTY words, rich with significance! Jesus affirms His identity with the everlasting God who gave His name to Moses as the Infinite Being, self-caused, without beginning and without end, Jehovah! "I am the Alpha and the Omega, the beginning and the end . . . who is and who was and who is coming, the Almighty." Before Abraham, everywhere and with everyone, in the uttermost parts of the sea, in the heights of heaven, beyond the bounds of uncharted space, God is, and was, and always will be.

In this world inhabited by men, whose minds are so often saturated with personal interests and temporal affairs, there is, as the poet sensed, a divine reality, "A presence not to be put by." God the heavenly Father, the Son, the Holy Spirit—has right to an unassailable priority. The first place belongs to Him. His interests must be taken into account before all others. Otherwise human affairs will be totally disordered. The world will be out of joint. We may be moving incessantly; but paths irrationally chosen can end only in chaos.

I know that of all the issues which may concern me there is none comparable in importance to this: Is my soul aware of Your Presence? Is my will adjusted to Your Will? I turn to You, dear Master and Lord, to say in unison with all Your children: May there be glory to God on high and on earth peace to men of good will! For You are the only-begotten Son, Jesus Christ, Lord God, Lamb of God, Son of the Father, who taketh away the sin of the world! Have mercy on us. Receive our prayers. Have mercy on us!

If Thou Didst Know the Gift of God (John 4, 10)

DEEPEST of man's instincts is his hunger for God. It is an instinct that may be distorted, that may for a time be ignored, suppressed. But it is identical with man's irrepressible longing for total and enduring happiness; and he cannot live peacefully, hopefully, even sanely, unless he knows that he is making use of his resources to attain God. Only the Infinite One can satisfy our longing for truth and beauty and holiness.

The revelation of God in the Incarnation is an unfailing source of encouragement and strength to the soul. Through paths of divine friendship the faithful disciple is led to heights where he may enjoy a communion immeasurably more dear than life itself. Not merely has he set eyes upon a model of human perfection, lovely enough to dazzle the beholder; not only has he found the truest of true friends. He has, in this moment of privileged intimacy, even begun to taste the wonderful reality of God's love; to satisfy, at least in part, the yearning of man for his Maker; to attain a certain vision of the divinity, though at present God is seen as in a glass, darkly.

Because I have been taught these truths and because Your grace has enabled me to believe them, I thank You with all my heart. Dear Lord, I will try not to disgrace the name of disciple which You allow me to bear; and I will try to help others to share in these blessed privileges which belong to every Catholic Christian. In union with them I will keep saying: We praise You; we bless You; we adore You; we glorify You. We give You thanks for Your great glory, O Lord God, heavenly King, God the Father Almighty!

I Am the Living Bread (John 6, 51)

WE CAN hardly mention banquet or feast or supper table without thinking immediately of the Last Supper when Our Lord gave Himself for the first time to His disciples, to be to them the Bread of Life. We who from childhood have been familiar with the idea of Communion, find it hard to realize how startling the notion is to others less fortunate than ourselves. Communion implies actual incorporation with Jesus, an embrace of the soul and God. And a persuasive argument for the divine origin of the Church might be built out of her success in bringing countless multitudes to unquestioning belief in Holy Communion and to an eager desire for it.

Holy Communion effects contact of spirit with Spirit. On the part of the divine Lover there is gracious, generous giving; on our part, grateful, humble, loyal return. From Him comes a lifting up, purifying, ennobling of the worshiping soul; from us goes an appeal for pardon and aid, a bending of the knee in adoration, a grasping of His outstretched hand, a touching of Him with reverential lips. The motive for frequent Communion becomes plain once we realize that each new reception of the sacrament is a renewal of affection, a confirmation of mutual pledges already given.

Dear Lord, every time I receive Holy Communion, or even when I see another worshiper approach You at the altar rail, I seem to be given a sharp reminder of my duty. I must intensify my consciousness of Your Presence. I must take faster hold of Your Will. Like all sinners, I dislike to be reminded of neglected opportunities. But, on the other hand, I long to fulfill more generously my obligations to You. May that longing never be interrupted!

19th WEEK AFTER PENTECOST—SATURDAY
This Is the Bread That Comes Down From Heaven
(John 6, 50)

OF SOME saints it has been said that their day was divided between thanksgiving for the Communion last made and preparation for the Communion to come. If a man's faith were strong enough to make him see things as he will see them in eternity, he would gladly spend his time in this double activity of thanking and of making ready. Those of us who go to the altar daily may well confess that we exercise our spiritual sight too little. Our bodily eyes are roving about or intent on objects attractive to sense. The eyes of faith grow feeble through misuse. Our vision is dim; our will is weak.

When we are preparing for Communion and whenever we assist at Mass, we should try, for the moment at least, to set aside earthly, selfish human interests—especially those which are in any degree discordant with God's Will. We should dedicate ourselves to the fulfilling of the heavenly Father's plans. We should take Our Lord's point of view, think His thoughts, make His Will ours. For us He should be the center of the universe; and the importance of anything to us should be identical with its importance to Him.

Dear Lord and Master, would that I could realize the shocking contrast between what I am and what I should be. I begin to see what is happening as the days of my life rush past. Time is wasted. My fate is being decided. Heaven may be lost! I have set You and Your Will and Your interests in a corner of my day, as things of lesser importance, and devoted my time to more material items. Father, Son and Holy Spirit, and you, too, O Blessed Mother, help me henceforth to prepare well for Communion and to remain under its inspiration lastingly!

Thy Son . . . Lives (John 4, 50)

AFTER Jesus had restored health to the ruler's son, the father and all his household "found faith." Here again, as on so many other occasions, we find Our Lord coming to the aid of the afflicted—the cripple at the pool, the man who was deaf and dumb, the man with the withered hand, the man with dropsy, the men possessed by evil spirits, the ailing woman, the ten lepers. The blessed memories that Our Lord left with us will serve to reassure Christians until the end of time.

In dealing with the helpless and the needy, Jesus made those who witnessed His miracles—and also us who read about them— aware that the finest and most inspiring deeds of men reflect the attributes of the heavenly Father. The wonders that He wrought display His possession of qualities which we instinctively recognize as divine. In this impressive fashion, He enables us to perceive that God's image has already been stamped upon human nature; and that it can be developed to perfection only by the exercise of the virtues which He practiced during His life on earth. These virtues may be summed up by saying that, in His dealing with men, He was divinely kind; and that His attitude toward His heavenly Father was one of uninterrupted and wholehearted worship.

From my childhood, dear Lord, I have known of the blessed deeds which demonstrated Your love of mankind. As I grew older, I learned about Your perfect union with the heavenly Father in mind and will. Your dealing with the unhappy and the unfortunate stamps upon my consciousness the conviction that I must love and serve my neighbor; Your inner habit of contemplation spells out for me the secret of moral beauty and divine holiness. It all adds up to an ideal which I see is the only goal really worthy of human striving. Help me, then, dear Lord and Master, to reflect the characteristics which You displayed during Your earthly life; for I know they must be shared, at least to some extent, by any person worthy of the name of Christian.

I Am in Your Midst as He Who Serves (Luke 22, 27)

IT REQUIRES no extraordinary intelligence to perceive that pride often occasions evil. But comparatively few men see that pride is at the root of *all* evil; for they do not identify pride under the clever disguises which it assumes. This is the reason why we are slow to credit the statement that self-love, not sex, was the primary motive that led our first parents to sin. And we are astonished when we hear a saint declare that Mary Magdalen's development into sanctity was less surprising than the holiness of highly gifted intellectual genius like Aquinas.

Let us make no mistake about it. The root of evil is pride. "By that sin fell the angels!" Nature does not like to hear that man has no possessions except those loaned to him; that we are dependent; that our freedom is a concession and our rights are privileges. Pride moves us to see in ourselves something that is not really there. We focus attention upon our temporary possessions and turn a blind eye to God's infinity. The expression of practically all our sinful behavior is that we live in a fantastic, unreal world—within the aura of our projected ego.

Dear Lord, I remember Your words "I was watching Satan fall as lightning from Heaven." Behind all my weaknesses and evil-doing lies my wretched unwillingness to face reality, to admit my total dependence, to accept my limitations and obligations. Even when I seem least arrogant, I am often moved by "the pride that apes humility." Even when I appear to be well disciplined, generous, regular in the discharge of my spiritual duties, frequently, I fear, I do "the right deed for the wrong reason." Were it not for Your grace, dear Lord, I should despair of overcoming this weakness; but at Your bidding and because of Your encouragement, I will keep up the struggle!

You Hypocrites! (Luke 12, 56)

THE self-styled "elect" are egotists who have been caricatured in the phrase "I am holier than thou!" They are odious to men. What is more important, they are odious to God. Inordinate self-esteem is so obvious a contradiction of the Gospel ideal that we wonder how anyone can be blind to its essentially unchristian quality. The ridiculous assumption of superiority may be the result of a wish to conform to the common code of worldliness; it may come from one's own imagined spiritual excellence; or it may be a prompting of constitutional meanness, or envy, or some other form of egotism.

The point to be considered is that any such egotistical characteristic defaces the image of Christ within the soul. One who would be like Christ must not draw back from communion with sinners who need help, even if association with them will bring the disapproval of companions. There is a vivid contrast between the over righteous Pharisee, hard, cold, unsympathetic, and the humble saint who says, "I am not conscious to myself of anything, yet am I not hereby justified." We have the teaching of Scripture that humility is the way to glory, and that pride is the great danger. St. Paul, with all his indomitable will, gives unmistakable proofs of possessing that spirit of lowliness which changes the mighty ones of earth into the likeness of little children.

Let me see clearly, dear Lord, the antagonism between Your Spirit and the spirit of the world. On many other points a sort of compromise will be offered, or at least permitted, by the world; but not humility. Yet this ideal of Your Gospel successfully stands the test of experiment and fulfills its promise. The men and women who have been humble are the only men and women who have attained real greatness. Help me, then, to remember that it will really do me no great or lasting harm if the world looks scornfully upon me as it looked upon Christ and says, "This man receiveth sinners!"

If You Abide in My Word, You Shall . . .
Know the Truth (John 8, 31-32)

HUMILITY is the child of simplicity and the parent of sanctity. It urges undivided attention to the one thing needful. It sweeps aside the petty interests of earth. What is divine and splendid is bought with the surrender of what is known to be paltry and valueless, be it ever so shining. The pearl of great price is eagerly purchased; all lesser jewels are gladly sold. The truly humble man will be necessarily holy; and the saint will possess true humility.

It is safe to say that few of us habitually realize how far we are from being humble. Few of us appreciate the steps we need to cultivate the virtue of lowliness and to practice the ideals we profess. The false lights of the world tend to blind us; but the soul whose eyes are bent steadily upon the Crucified Jesus will not be led astray.

Do You, dear Lord, teach me much about the world and about myself. Let me learn that humility does not consist in the exaggeration of my own defects or the minimizing of my own virtues; it does not begin and end with advancing the interests of others at my own expense; it is not to be acquired by talking in deprecatory fashion of the things which men naturally hold in high esteem. Rather, it is based upon a true view of the proportion between things human and things divine; and thus it makes ridiculous all talk of my own importance. Humbled to the level of my own nothingness, distrusting my own shortsighted vision, I shall be enabled to see with the penetrating vision of God. The straight path to the virtue of humility is the practice of contemplating You!

Dost Thou Believe in the Son of God? (John 9, 35)

OUR Lord taught us the beauty of serving our fellowmen. His own life is so shining an example of it
that many see no higher significance in His Gospel than
a summons to what they call social service. They find
the essence of Christianity in the Golden Rule; they tell
us that the only immortality we can attain is an immortality of influence which will persist forever in lives
made nobler because of us. Our memorial will be a cup
of strength offered to others in some great agony, after
we ourselves shall have joined the choir invisible "whose
music is the gladness of the world."

Faith teaches a doctrine quite different from this.
The life of the visible Christ was for the effecting of an
invisible revolution whereby individual souls would be
fitted to live eternally with God. Most potent element in
human history is the divine grace which effects the transformation of the natural into the supernatural. So far
as the two things can be compared, the service of God
is immeasurably more important than the service of
man. The future, not the present, the life of Heaven, not
the life of earth, is to be the goal of all our striving.

The Incarnation brought You, dear Lord, into more
intimate companionship with the sons of men than had
ever before been possible. Ways of dealing that the
world approves of, and that I myself once admired,
shrivel up into pettiness and meanness when I consider
how they look to You. The law which regulates buying
and selling in shop and market seems barbaric when I
remember You, who erected such different rules of conduct for Your disciples. Let me never forget that You
are here present, waiting to see whether I shall be loyal
of heart or a traitor to Your example. If I remember
that You are looking at me, I am very apt to behave as
You would wish!

I Say to You Not to Resist the Evildoer (Matt. 5, 39)

CLARITY of vision comes to the humble man. He does not suffer his soul to be tormented by issues that fret and trouble others. He knows it is not a matter of eternal concern to have his opinion accepted as final, and his will recognized as dominant. There is but one good, God alone. There is but One who has the right to claim attention, obedience, reverence. It is of little account that the rest of us should have to wait, or be misunderstood, or be treated unfairly.

But this habit of patience does not come easily to us who are selfish by instinct, and undisciplined by custom —more anxious to get than to give. It is hard for us to undertake the great adventure of abandoning our all and counting it as nothing. It is hard for us to employ our time, and spend our money, and shape our efforts, and point our prayers, as if we believed that our chief, and indeed our only, concern was to carry out the Will of God; as if we were possessed by an overmastering desire to cultivate love for God and neighbor at the cost of postponing everything else.

Dear Lord, may I have the grace to understand how selfishly I behave when I am threatened by some sort of "evil." I know it is not a sufficient excuse for me to say that I have been humiliated, or annoyed, or disappointed, or overworked. It is my business to train myself in the exercise of those habits which St. Paul describes as the attributes of love. I must become patient, kind, unsuspicious; I must tirelessly bear all things; and I must never fall away!

I Will Draw All Things to Myself (John 12, 32)

OUR Lord's first disciples were slow to grasp the significance of His words—teachings that are plain enough to us who look back at His revelation through the clarifying history of twenty centuries. But that first generation, and indeed several following generations, came only haltingly to an appreciation of what His words implied. Toward human slowness and dullness, He was always infinitely patient—as in His dealing with the doubting Thomas.

A skillful teacher states a truth plainly and then elaborates what he has said, giving concrete illustrations for the benefit of his pupils. Thus slow-moving minds are gradually adjusted; they are not disturbed by being jostled or hurried. At last the light dawns. The truth is seen. The favorite prescription of St. Francis de Sales was "Honey, not vinegar." In my efforts to win souls to God—whether Catholics or non-Catholics—gentleness and patience will always be good medicine.

Dear Lord, I am grateful to You for Your patience. I shall try to train myself in this virtue; and I rely upon Your grace to help me. I must meditate on You, always considerate of the weak and always long-suffering with the dull. I must not be hasty, spilling out ill-chosen words, or showing bad temper. May Your example move me to restrain my speech and curb my impulses, when I have to deal with those who are moving toward the truth more slowly than I would wish and perhaps more painfully than I realize. Were I more like You, and like all other patient teachers, I should be able to help souls more effectively.

Wicked Servant (Matt. 18, 32)

YEAR after year, as this text is read, the wicked servant is pilloried in all the churches of the world. He is a man with a double standard. To be exacting, quick to condemn, cruel, is bad enough; but to beg successfully for mercy for one's self and then refuse it to another, this seems to everybody unpardonable. One should do as one would be done by. We find no words strong enough to express our disapproval; so we sit in judgment on this man and reflect that he was properly punished.

The story of the wicked servant is, however, a parable. In other words, it contains a moral, a lesson for us to meditate upon. You and I should note the outstanding characteristics of the wicked servant and then ask ourselves whether or not we resemble him. Are *we* willing to be judged by the same standards that we employ in passing judgment upon our neighbors? Or do we allow ourselves to commit the faults that we condemn in others? Do we seek privileges that we do not like to see extended to anyone else? Do we offer excuses that we would reject as inadequate, if they were presented to us? These are points for self-examination which may well be pondered by us as we review all the various human relationships which we possess—with companions, neighbors, friends, strangers, enemies, persons above us, persons below us, persons on the same level with us, persons from whom we anticipate favors and persons from whom we have received injuries.

Dear Lord, I know how dear to You is the straightforward speech of the honest man who has the same name for the same deed, whether performed by himself or by another, by a friend or by an enemy. I know that it will cost me much to speak and act in accord with Your ideal of unselfishness; but I know, too, that eventually it will cost me much more to act in any other way. Here, as always, my best interests are identical with Your wishes. Help me to be as You wish me to be, not like the wicked servant!

So Also My Heavenly Father Will Do to You, If You Do Not Each Forgive Your Brothers from Your Hearts
(Matt. 18, 35)

THE conventions of civilized life call for a certain amount of give and take between man and man. One must accept a frank apology; one must pardon another who makes excuses for an indeliberate affront; one must meet an opponent halfway in an offer of reconciliation. But the laws of the kingdom of Heaven establish a far higher standard; they call for much more in the way of self-restraint and forgiveness. For mere social conduct is regulated by the rule of common decency, whereas spiritual behavior must conform to a nobler, more difficult ideal. I must forgive the man who still hates me. I must wish well to those from whose injustice I still suffer. I must go to the uttermost limit in seeking reconciliation. I must return good for evil.

How few of us take these obligations quite literally—to smile, to speak graciously, to forget as well as forgive, to act so that observers would not detect any difference in our tone, whether we are dealing with friends, or with rivals, or with enemies. How many there are, who would shudder at the thought of receiving Holy Communion with a sin of dishonesty or impurity or blasphemy on their souls, who yet dare approach the altar, with hearts full of anger and hatred, and bring Our Lord into a place that He abhors—an unforgiving heart.

Let me recall, dear Lord, the stinging rebukes You aimed at the merciless. Remind me of the exhortations to charity and mutual love that were always on Your lips. Let me realize that I must be with You or against You; I must either heed You or despise You. I must try, at all costs, to be charitable; or I shall have no part with You!

Dost Thou Love Me? (John 21, 15)

THE question that Our Lord addressed to St. Peter will be addressed to each one of us. Only because Peter could answer "Yes" was he fit to be entrusted with the care of Christ's flock. Only if we can give the right answer shall we be worthy of admission into the kingdom of Heaven. This fact may remind us that love is a prerequisite for anyone who is about to undertake a divine task. The essential element in the equipment of the apostle, the priest, the parent, the lay worker, is not primarily intellectual, or physical; it is moral and spiritual. If we are to deserve the name of Christian, we must be ready to radiate the spirit of Christ toward all, near or far, including those who dislike us and those who grate upon us; and we must be ready to do this as missionaries are ready to love and serve the heathen in far off distant lands. Therefore we had better be sure we are at least promising apprentices in the art of loving.

We can best understand the meaning of sin when we think of it as the opposite of love. True love is a rare phenomenon; it is rare because human beings—often unconsciously and secretly— are victims of inordinate self-esteem. Holiness is to give God His place and to put ourselves in our own place. And this is precisely what we do, if we learn the lesson of love. We receive great spiritual illumination the moment we discover that the reason we do not progress in the path of holiness is identical with the reason why we are not yet really capable of love.

I have been like St. Peter in his weakness. May I be like him in fervent repentance and in lifelong loyalty to You, dear Lord. May I realize that God is all and that we are ourselves nothing. The saints—greatest lovers in the history of mankind—were personifications of humility; and the habitual way in which they expressed themselves was by loving. This is harking back to first principles; this is disclosing the secret that all of us claim we wish to learn—how to love as Our Lord loves!

In Me You May Have Peace (John 16, 33)

HUMANITY dreams of the peace about which the angels sang at the birth of Christ. Next to the glory of God, its attainment motivated Our Lord's coming. *Beata visio,* the blessed vision of peace, is the source of the soul's blessedness in Heaven. And so unquenchable is man's yearning for peace, that even those who make war put forth as their motive the ultimate establishment of peace. We should not be surprised then, if any book which promises the reader peace of mind attains an amazing circulation. But men who are in peril of being lured away from ancient wisdom by the appeal of novelty would do well to reconsider the Christian teaching on the subject of peace.

A passage of the *Imitation of Christ* represents Our Lord as directing the attention of His disciple to four rules which bring peace: "Rather do the will of another than thine own"; "Choose to have less rather than more"; "Seek the lowest place"; "Wish and pray that God's Will may be entirely fulfilled in thee." No one who looks at this outline can fail to see how sharply it contrasts with the advice given by most of those who are undertaking to help man or nations toward peace today. An acute observer may be hopeless about winning multitudes to the pursuit of the ideals described in the *Imitation of Christ;* but he will quite readily agree that, if these ideals were faithfully observed, men's souls would not easily be troubled.

Let me, dear Lord, obey the four rules attributed to You in that wise book. Give me the grace to conform to the principles there set forth. May I thus "learn to disregard the evil thoughts and fears that afflict my soul; may I find hope and comfort by having recourse to You in all tribulation; may I confide in You during every trial; and may I always patiently look to You for comfort and for peace!"

He Will Convict the World of Sin (John 16, 8)

THE world today shows widening reluctance to accept Our Lord's teaching on sin. That reluctance comes as an almost inevitable result of popular theories which point to the disturbing effect of what is called "a guilt complex." Ill-behaved men are urged to seek a peace of mind, first by analyzing the circumstances which provoke undesirable emotions and then by rearranging those circumstances as far as possible. Not in sorrow for wrong doing, not in humble petition for pardon, not in firm resolution to avoid sinful occasions, but by confidently dwelling on our own self-sufficiency are we to attain peace—so we are told.

The essential mistake of ignoring sin is that this procedure takes no heed of a universal, deep-seated instinct of our nature, and that it contradicts human experience. It is a closing of the mind to what conscience tells every man. It is a denial of the reality which impresses itself upon every unspoiled soul. It is "crying peace, where there is no peace"—a repudiating of hardwon moral achievement, a suppressing of the difference between selfish and heroic conduct, a confusing of judgment whereby we equalize what is degraded with what is sublime. It imagines a world, where there is no sin, no prayer, no worship, no God, no responsibility, no basis for self-accusation, no ultimate difference between right and wrong. Advice of this sort is more palatable to the sinner than the traditional teaching; but it is far less effective. And nothing in the contemporary scene indicates that it is either as true or as helpful in restoring peace of mind as Christian teaching has been.

Help me, dear Lord, to keep my mind open to all the new discoveries that may be made by those who minister to ills of mind and body. Help me still more to adjust thoughts and behavior to Your ideal of repentance, amendment, self-denial, prayer. The Psalmist taught me to esteem the value of the contrite and the humble heart. You set the stamp of Your approval on this teaching; and I will follow it!

They Would Have Repented Long Ago (Luke 10, 13)

EVERY so often something suggests that we stop short and consider the value of habits we have been cultivating. Today we are challenged as to whether or not we can discern the Presence and the Will of God amid appearances that repel the worldly-minded man. Naturally, a man desires what is pleasant and beautiful— comfort, wealth, friendship, influence. He shrinks from what is poor. But in turning away he often loses his best opportunity of doing God's Will and of receiving a divine reward.

The daily practice of penance would train and prepare us for such opportunities, would save us from the disaster of rejecting God's grace when offered in lowly guise. Light and strength, piercing vision and power of will result from long continued self-denial. The world counts for little with the man who has acquired the habit of renunciation. On the other hand, a man accustomed to self-indulgence will sometimes condone or approve moral blunders and grave crimes.

My neighbors may not help me by their example; they may even mock at my foolishness. You have made plain, dear Lord, that there is no smooth path, no broad avenue, no level road to Heaven. If I am to be like You, I must steel myself to endure tribulation patiently, to accept disappointments serenely, to persevere in the face of discomfort or disapproval. With St. Thomas More then, I pray:

Give me grace, good God,
To set the world at naught,
To be content to be solitary,
To bewail my sins passed,
To be joyful in tribulations,
To walk the narrow path that leadeth to life.

What Is It to Thee? (John 21, 22)

THERE is much wisdom in the homely proverb "Mind your own business." It may even be regarded as a perfect rule of conduct and a road to holiness—if a man has the correct idea of his "business" and an heroic determination to "mind"it. What trouble and unhappiness he would avoid if he lived according to the implications of this proverb!

A little book that puts this lesson before the reader convincingly is Caussade's *Abandonment*. Its teaching may be summed up as follows: Since nothing can happen except by God's permission, and since He permits nothing really destructive of His own purpose, we may abandon ourselves with perfect confidence to the working out of any situation in which we find ourselves. Nothing and nobody can keep us from fulfilling His Will and attaining happiness; indeed, there is nothing and nobody that cannot be utilized as an aid to our progress. This general truth holds good with regard to the past, the present, the future. It includes the experiences of the body and of the soul—blessings and burdens, joy and pain, friendship and persecution. It is our chief business —in the highest sense, our only business—to take toward every creature and every occurrence precisely the attitude which seems to accord with the Will of God.

Once again, dear Lord, I resign myself to whatever You allow to happen. It is not necessary for me to be able to foretell the practical consequences of any choice of mine or any action; it is enough that I choose what, so far as I can see, is in accord with Your Will. Then I can go on my way serene and confident. Come to the aid of my too self-conscious and therefore often frightened soul. Teach me to rely on You, not on myself or on any other. To the dispensations of Your Providence I commit myself unreservedly, even when that implies my encounter with things that are menacing and terrifying. In You I have hoped. I shall not be left helpless!

Render ... to God the Things That Are God's
(Matt. 22, 21)

THIS is a balanced statement. God demands of us only that which belongs to Him—nothing more. The claim cannot reasonably be denied. Yet human beings find it hard to be perfectly reasonable. They have a distorted idea of the universe; for they magnify out of all due proportion that part of the world with which they come into immediate contact. Sometimes it seems that all the things and all the persons near at hand are in a conspiracy to make us forget the unseen provinces of God's dominions. Many creatures look and act as if they belong to me; they do my bidding. I have power to influence and direct the activities of other men. The very laws of nature wait upon me. Space is mine to move about wheresoever I will; time is mine to spend as I choose.

What then is God's due? How much should we give Him in order not to cheat Him of anything that is truly His? Obviously, if we believe in God at all, we must admit that in the last analysis everything belongs to Him. We have nothing that does not come to us as a gift, a loan, a "talent" held in trust, to be accounted for later. To satisfy the demands of justice, therefore, man must spend no moment of time, use no faculty of body or mind, dispose of no created thing, animate or inanimate, except in accord with the Will of his Creator.

Of all this I am reminded by that most reasonable principle which You have formulated, dear Lord. Once again I recall that I am but a steward, a servant. Whatever I have or control belongs to You. It must all be used for You, in some way given to You; for in very truth it is Your own. Only when I am using everything according to Your Will am I leading a well-ordered life. Only then may I properly be called a reasonable being. Only then am I rendering to God the things that are God's; and this is what I will try to do!

Render . . . to Caesar the Things
That Are Caesar's (Matt. 22, 21)

THE Pharisees had framed a crafty question: Is it lawful to contribute to Caesar? There were reasons why a conscientious Jew might presumably scruple about the payment of tribute to the Romans. First, because it was a recognition of Roman authority; also, because tribute had to be paid in coin bearing the graven image of the Roman emperor. In solving the case of conscience presented to Him, Our Lord affirmed a principle valid for all time—the principle which regulates the whole relationship of man and state. Civil authority derives from God and, within proper limitations, binds in conscience; but civil law must always harmonize with the moral law. No act of a temporal power may ignore God or violate the inalienable rights of man.

Whenever man's instinctive respect for legitimate authority grows weak, this deplorable condition results at least in part from the tendency of rulers to overstep the limits established by natural law. In season and out of season, the Church impresses upon the conscience of all her children the importance of the moral bulwark against totalitarian encroachments. Her teaching is no less necessary in the twentieth century than it was in Our Lord's time.

I recognize, dear Lord, that as a matter of conscience I must render obedience to civil law when it issues from legitimate authority and remains within due limits. I recognize, too, the duty of denying the claim and resisting the efforts of any ruler who disregards the rights of the individual. Christians must play their part in public life. They must defend with their words and with their votes the true theory of government and the conscientious representatives of authority. For it is a wrong thing to misuse authority; and wrong to support those who misuse it.

My Kingdom Is Not of This World (John 18, 36)

THERE are two sides to this. Our Lord proclaims His indifference to those things which form the basis of worldly greatness—the ends to which the mass of men direct their desires, plans, labors. The worldling in turn—although he may pay the idle compliment of a verbal tribute to Christian ideals—repudiates in practice the principles that Our Lord imposed upon His disciples. There is a vital, fundamental opposition between the two patterns of conduct—not the less vital for being secret and undeclared. One cannot serve God and the world.

The Jesus who rejected worldly maxims of prudence in the Sermon on the Mount, who refused to provide for the morrow by gathering silver and gold, who would not condone the injustice of the powerful or give them priority over the poor and weak—this same Jesus proved that His kingdom could not be overcome when, in defiance of the Jewish mob and the Roman soldiers, He stood before the high priest and in the court of Pilate. Quietly He affirmed His ability to overcome His enemies, had He so wished, by asking His Father for legions of angels. The world could not vanquish Him; it could not even make Him fear.

Dear Lord, I am beginning to learn that to belong to Your kingdom, I must part company with the world; I must repudiate its code of conduct. But, although I often pledge allegiance to You, I fear I am disloyal many times when I am tempted. I need to be frequently and forcibly reminded that spiritual progress is measured by the number and variety of the sacrifices one is willing to make. I must surrender what I never thought I should have to give up. I see You meant what You said about the Cross: The approach to holiness is along the pathway of self-denial; love is attained through renunciation.

22nd WEEK AFTER PENTECOST—WEDNESDAY
Woe to You Rich (Luke 6, 24)

WE DO not at first realize the significance of this censure passed on the rich. It implies a definite cleavage between them, with their purple and fine linen, their pride of place, their claim to privilege, their love of comfort, and the Son of Man who had no place to lay His head, who was poorer than the foxes of the field and the birds of the air. Poverty runs like a theme through His life and teaching.

Let us not quibble about the word "riches." It stands for things naturally desirable—food, clothing, shelter, comfort, protection against illness and weather and vermin and dirt. This leads us to consider our possible resemblance to the class described in the Gospel as rich. We may have little likeness to them so far as money is concerned; nevertheless we may occupy a position which is far more comfortable than that of the privileged wealthy class two thousand years ago. It is an axiom in spiritual science that ease and comfort tend to soften character; that it is good for a man when he bears the yoke from his youth. This raises the suspicion that many of us who have little ready cash may suffer from the characteristic maladies of the rich.

Dear Lord, I fear that I am in large degree attached to food and clothing and comfort; that I am not, either in external conditions or in spirit, like the multitude around me, ill-fed, ill-housed, ill-clothed. I know that too rarely do I search my conscience on this point. Therefore I now resolve to examine myself about it more frequently and more carefully in the future.

FOR AGES the poor widow has served as a model of unaffected simplicity. We, who so often hang back less through modesty than through human respect, find in her a symbol of desirable qualities that are lacking in us. Able to offer only a negligible trifle, she comes forward to give it, showing no hesitation, offering no apology, troubled by no mean wishes or subtle envy. She does not even wait until everyone else has gone away. A trained psychologist might say that she gave no evidence of being frustrated and that, on this account, she remained more nearly normal than the rest of us; for we often shrink away from the doing of our simple duty because the splendid activities of other persons leave us with a paralyzing sense of inferiority.

We, who assume a humble pose, may be giving in to suggestions that come from secret, possibly unconscious, egotism. Not having been chosen to act as leaders and not possessing the qualification of leadership, we think it better not to march in the procession at all. Because we cannot match the generous gifts of wealthy neighbors, we give nothing. Sometimes we are tongue-tied, shy, dumb, because we weakly yield to the pressure of fears that we should long ago have trained ourselves to overcome.

Dear Lord, as I meditate upon the conduct of the poor widow, I see quite plainly a lesson that is greatly needed by me. I should not be moved either to act or to desist from acting, by the consideration of what people will think. I should be concerned only with the one question: Shall I have Your approval or disapproval? May I learn the lesson of giving You what I now have, instead of waiting until I get more. May I be less self-conscious, less complicated, much more direct and simple. If I am a little like the poor widow, I know I shall be at least a little pleasing to You.

If Thy Eye Is An Occasion of Sin to Thee, Pluck It Out
(Matt. 18, 9)

THESE are startling, alarming words. They convey a lesson very hard to learn, namely, that pain—even agonizing pain—is to be preferred to sinful pleasures. They teach that the deliberate misuse of God's gift is a greater evil than its loss. To turn a blessing into the instrument of evil is an act of perversion—a loathsome word that has come to be associated with sexual offences, although it literally fits every open-eyed, deliberate sin. The beginning of moral wisdom consists in knowing that it is better to lack a gift of God than to misuse it. While we do our feeble best, He aids us to struggle on; but if we set our will against His, He will block our way. Then, sooner or later, we shall be crushed. Happier the paralytic than the fleet runner heading for the gates of hell.

The world in which we live is filled with God's abundant gifts. But we must not be deluded into the notion that we are at liberty to exploit the world and its contents in behalf of ourselves and our friends. Man, who has a supernatural destiny, must develop into more than man or become less. The horizon of earth is not a boundary but a gateway to Heaven. That which satiates the animal nature will easily corrode the soul. The highest value that attaches to material goods is the opportunity they offer us for the exercise of self-denial. What is relinquished here will be regained a hundredfold hereafter.

Teach me then, dear Lord, that self-interest must never be the motive of my conduct. I am to be primarily concerned with spiritual, eternal, supernatural aims. I must not resemble the unbeliever who ignores the universal dominion of his Creator; nor must I be like those fickle inconsistent, nominal disciples who recognize the supremacy of Your claims, yet refuse to give You what is clearly Yours. It was to such as these that You said, "If you were blind, you would not have sin; but now that you say: We see, your sin remains."

He . . . Shall Never Thirst (John 4, 13)

MORE than once Our Lord promised His disciples that they would drink of the heavenly water which gives eternal life. The Scriptures often present water as a symbol of that precious gift from God without which the soul must perish—a figure of speech especially significant in tropical countries where water is highly prized and where everybody understands that dehydration is the equivalent of death. Our Lord's promise implied that He would offer a perfect pattern of life to souls confused. His teaching on self-denial, honesty, purity, prayer appealed to man's instinctive love of good; He presented the impressive argument that to follow Him would mean to gain all, whereas to reject Him would would mean to lose all. But many of those who crowded about Him, shouting His praises and trying to make Him king, soon fell away from Him under the influence of human apathy, the lust of the flesh, the fear of pain, "the pride of life."

The history of Christianity presents us with the record of countless individuals, families, peoples whose virtue reflects honor on the name they bear. But we find, too, that a pagan spirit, wearing the garments and bearing the name of Christianity, has often led multitudes to forsake the fountain of Christ's doctrine, to repudiate practical belief in the supremacy of the spiritual and in the value of self-denial. In our own day this spirit is very active; and we should remind ourselves that, unless the soul drinks at the fountain of Our Lord's teaching, it can no more live than the body without water.

Dear Lord, let me open my mind and my heart to the living water which You offer for my soul's refreshment. Would that I could give myself to You by constant remembrance, by deep devotedness, by that unique degree of love which we call adoration. Then I would spend much time meditating on the Gospels; then I would study the lives and read the writings of the saints.

The Girl Is . . . Not Dead (Matt. 9, 24)

IN ANSWER to her father's prayer, Our Lord raised the ruler's daughter to life again. This was one of those "cosmic" miracles which were plain interventions in the established order of nature — for example, changing water into wine, walking upon the waters, stilling the tempest, withering the fig tree. Miracles of this sort hold so conspicuous a place in the Gospel story that to eliminate them would be to devitalize the narrative. Yet, on the other hand, Our Lord did not wish to build the faith of His disciples chiefly on "signs and wonders"; He refused to be publicized as a wonder-working Messiah.

In our scientific age some persons refuse to believe in the possibility of miracles, because they contradict the laws of nature. This is a superficial objection. Even men can intervene in the operation of natural laws. It seems plain that the Creator of nature can do much more than this. The Church requires belief in the historical fact that certain miracles have occurred. Further, to deny the occurrence of miracles since the time of Christ is to disregard the laws of evidence and to attack the honesty and intelligence of persons, well qualified to bear witness, who give testimony to what they have personally seen.

Dear Lord, I recall the message that You gave the disciples of John the Baptist to carry back to their master: "Go and report to John what you have heard and seen: the blind see, the lame walk, the lepers are cleansed." Thus You drew attention to the fact that the wonders You wrought were proof of Your mission from the Father. I believe that You are the Son of God. I know that, as You said, all power is given to You in Heaven and earth; and I find no difficulty in believing that You are the Omnipotent Master of both the visible and the invisible world. I believe that the Father is in You and You are in the Father; and I believe the works You do—all of them. I wish to be totally unlike those who approach the evidence of Your miracles with cynical irreverence. I am grateful to You for the revelation You have made of Your power!

I Give Them Everlasting Life (John 10, 28)

"ASPIRATIONS of Nature" and "Questions of the Soul" are suggestive phrases. They remind us that man was made for God; that his soul aspires to a happiness obtainable only in Heaven; that he is tormented by questions to which God alone gives the answer. Newman's story, "Callista," tells of a young Greek girl with an artist's love of beauty, with an instinctive longing for holiness. Those around her gave the advice: "Enjoy the present; leave nothing to the future!" Still unsatisfied, she kept searching, until she finally came to the knowledge of Christ through the reading of a copy of St. Luke's Gospel. This brought her into contact with One far removed from anything she had ever been able to imagine. Here was her ideal of perfection!

There is an ancient saying which describes the soul as "naturally Christian." It is an affirmation that the message of Jesus possesses an irresistible appeal to the unspoiled conscience. It suggests that there is a defect in anyone who can face perfection without being moved, who can look at truth and reject it, who can hear a summons to holiness and remain apathetic. Far worse than any merely intellectual weakness is the moral twist which keeps a man from appreciating the majestic personality of Our Lord and the persuasive truth of His doctrine.

Dear Lord, it is, I know, in reading and meditating upon the Gospel, in picturing Your deeds, in dwelling upon Your words, that I shall find my one chance to slake the thirst of my soul. From You and You alone, I learn effectively that I must sacrifice the present for the sake of the future. You have opened my eyes to the vision of God. You have taught me the answer to my questions; You satisfy my deepest longings!

He Who Believes in Me, Even If He Die, Shall Live
(John 11, 25)

To THE Christian there is immeasurable comfort in the doctrine of immortality. That doctrine serves as a background for all our achievement and aspirations, all our hopes, and all our fears. How consoling is the conviction that, if I believe truly in Our Lord, then through some mysterious process of cleansing and refining—partly in this life, partly in the next—I may hope to become fit for companionship not only with the saints but with God Himself. If I enter eternity after a life of faith, I shall begin a new life from which the very possibility of defilement, imperfection, or even temptation is excluded. This is my destiny.

The beginning of this eternal life comes through faith in Christ—faith which includes belief, explicit or implicit, in every truth that God has taught. It is not a blessing bestowed upon a passive soul; we must stretch out our hands to receive it. Once possessed, it proves to be the beginning of holiness—a divine gift, rich in possibilities; and, when developed, it effects constant communion and harmonious co-operation with the Omnipresent God.

Strengthen my faith, dear Lord, so that I may believe in the constant presence of the God who loves me, and for love's sake, lays a law upon me. O Lord, Creator of all things, I know that You are near me in every nook and corner of this visible world, near me in the midst of the big and little things that make up my daily life, always looking upon me, ever sounding the depths of my consciousness. You are appealing to me; and You are sensitive to my response, aware of my good conduct, or my ill-doing! This is indeed, the great fact of life; and constant attention to this fact is the basis of the greatest possible human holiness. It, and it alone, will bring me to that state where I shall be aware that You dwell within me; and I shall be made Your own forever!

Why Do You Harbour Evil Thoughts in Your Hearts?
(Matt. 9, 4)

To FIND fault is easy. It is so very easy that few of us keep wholly free from this often unjust, and nearly always demoralizing, form of self-indulgence. Our neighbor's imperfections are so obvious. There is no apparent reason to postpone unfavorable judgment. We find good excuses for criticizing and rebuking. Before we know it, we have developed a habit of picking on almost everyone who comes within our range of observation. We frequently wound charity. We are almost daily involved in recriminations and disputes.

It takes strength and wisdom for a man to restrain the impulses which urge him to assume some kind of superiority in dealing with his neighbor. Yet, you and I have known persons who, by dint of striving and prayer, have acquired the ability to control themselves; even when they note conduct that seems inexcusable, they refrain from passing judgment unless obliged to do so. Persons of this type are in marked contrast with those of us who quickly condemn whatever seems to merit censure and who go to great lengths in voicing condemnation.

Dear Lord, I will try not to be quick, not to be harsh, in my judgment of others. Perhaps it would be a good beginning for me to be a little quicker and harsher in the judgments I pass upon myself. The words of St. Paul keep echoing in my mind. He makes it plain that if I had charity—the greatest of all virtues—I should be patient and kind; I should be free from envy and ambition and self-seeking; I should not be suspicious. I have known a holy person to say that he would rather be imposed upon than to offend charity by looking into the possible deceit of another. This is the sort of clean-minded simplicity which we think of as characteristic of the saints. I shall hope, with the help of Your grace, to acquire some of it!

The Son of Man Has Power on Earth to Forgive Sins
(Matt. 9, 6)

THESE are consoling words. They remind us that sinners were the special object of God's coming to earth, and that, insofar as Our Lord showed special favor to anyone, it was to them. The memory of the methods He used keeps us from being startled at the way in which the Church deals with the sinner. Outspoken in the declaration of what God's law requires, uncompromising in denouncing guilt and threatening the guilty, she, nevertheless, with the same audacity that characterized Him, declares the pardon of the penitent and undertakes in God's name and with God's authority to soothe the contrite heart.

It is to the glory of the Church that she, like Christ, has been accused of keeping company with sinners. When the Puritan and the Pharisee find fault with her, her answer is the answer of Christ. She has been sent to the lost sheep. The sick need her ministrations, not those that are in health. It is not her mission to crush the bruised reed, or to quench the smoking flax; she comes to kindle in the soul the beginnings of sorrow and to fan into flame the still weak love of God. To all who are really penitent, the Church assures forgiveness, no matter how grave, nor how frequent, their sin.

Dear Lord, what blessing have I needed more than the conviction that You are ready to forgive me and take me back! It would be so easy to lose courage, when I find myself astray in the desert after having lost the road through my own foolishness. I would be terrified by the obstacles that I have myself created, were it not for my knowledge of Your goodness. Now for Your gift to me of fresh hope, new courage, I am grateful!

Behold My Mother and My Brethren (Mark 3, 34)

OUR Lord, paying an affectionate tribute to His disciples, named them His adopted family. Occasionally persons boast of noble lineage—a boast that has been well mocked in the couplet, "When Adam delved and Eve span, who was then the gentleman?" As for ourselves, to whom kinship with Eve has brought such woe, our membership in the family of saints gives us sound reasons for joy and gratitude. So it seems quite in order to meditate on this family of ours, beginning with its Mother, Our Blessed Lady. We picture this gracious being, who of all human persons was closest to God, as living now in Heaven; but we recall also that she actually lived and breathed in this world nineteen centuries ago; ate and slept and worked; smiled and spoke. This "woman above all women glorified" is the proudest boast of grace.

To Our Lady we pay a special worship, essentially lower than the adoration we pay to God, but higher than the veneration we give to the other members of Our Lord's family. With regard to them, we take much comfort and encouragement from the thought that all of us are united in a relationship, transcending time and space, which binds together the pure and the penitent, the scholar and the adventurer, the unknown orphan and the world-famed hero. We are stirred particularly by the reflection that most of the disciples who were gathered into the family by Our Lord Himself remain nameless and uncanonized.

Blessed Mother, you are so close to God that I can see Him reflected in you, His stainless handiwork! I see the divine glory reflected in you also, Angels and Saints of God! Holy Mary, pray for us. Saints and Angels intercede for us:

> For we do trust, by gracious bonds of prayer,
> Our souls are linked in such a wondrous wise,
> That no poor plea of ours, alone, need rise
> Before God's throne to sue for pardon there.

Seeing They Do Not See (Matt. 13, 13)

THERE is an old saying that all depends on the point of view. This, although an exaggeration, nevertheless conveys a truth. Variations in judgments about the same object come from training, prejudice, emotion, and many other sources. Ready illustrations may be found in the different impressions made by a sunset, a painting, a play, an automobile, on divers individuals such as an artist, a journalist, a mechanic, a scientist, a politician, a theologian. Philosophers tell us that things are received according to the nature and the condition of the recipient. When a man does not see what his neighbor sees, he may be at fault; or again he may be only unfortunate. Moralists classify mental blindness as culpable or inculpable, as sometimes vincible and sometimes invincible.

There are individuals who fail to see God in nature. Although "the heavens show forth the glory of God," comparatively few recognize the ever present source of this glory. A man may go through life blind to the significance of the shining stars, the dawn, the noon-day sun, the twilight shadows, the order and movement of the universe in spring, summer, autumn, winter. The soul blindness of some is like an impenetrable cloud; they are shamed by the saint who perceives not only the physical beauty in nature, but also God's presence there.

Let me, dear Lord and Master, always be sensitive to Your presence. May I respond instantly when the opportunity is given me to worship You. May I look at sun, and sky, and sea, and mountain, not as the pagan looks, but as the saint who goes through nature to nature's God. May I be aware of the constant displays of divine power and goodness which lie all around me. May I always see in them so many invitations to prayer, worship, adoration.

3rd WEEK AFTER EPIPHANY
PROVISIONAL MEDITATION—SUNDAY*
I Have Not Found Such Great Faith in Israel
(Matt. 8, 10)

IT is good for us to realize that those outside the pale often compare favorably with the children of the Kingdom. Christians may learn from non-Christians; Catholics from Protestants; the cloister may receive good example from the hearth; the pulpit from the pew. We, who are greatly blessed, cannot assume that our merit is necessarily equal to our privilege; that we are less open to temptation, or less strictly obliged to watch and pray and labor.

No one should have more confidence in God than the Christian. No one should be more patient. No one should be more humble. Yet we have to admit that persons outside the faith often show greater trust in God than we; that atheists are sometimes more zealous than believers, just as the crippled and the blind often accept hardship more graciously than the hale and hearty, just as a beggar may be less self-centered than a rich man. Knowing that it is a divine characteristic to recognize good wherever found, we should discover something to admire in the world of men; truth in every unfriendly criticism; an element of justice in every opponent's claim.

It sometimes happens that persons of wealth, social position, and culture, go wrong because they will not learn from others upon whom they look down. This attitude, of course, is foolish. A man's readiness to recognize distasteful truth is not only a disarming quality; it is a virtue, too—one that should be characteristic of Christ's disciples. May I, dear Lord, study the application of this idea to my daily life and to my ordinary relationships. May I acquire the habit of learning wisdom and goodness from everything and everybody..

---

* These Provisional Meditations are to be used as may be required in the weeks that intervene between the 23rd week after Pentecost and the last week of the Liturgical Year. See Note on page 94.

Unless You See Signs and Wonders, You Do Not Believe
(John 4, 48)

IN THE spiritual order as in the physical, some are keen of sight; and some are blind. Those who have dim vision, see only what is outstanding, conspicuous; they sense the grossness of murder, theft, adultery, and the madness of being impenitent. So, too, they are moved by the curing of a sightless man, by the raising of the dead. They find support and stimulus for their faith when they visit Lourdes, Molokai, Assisi. But to the beauty of poverty, humility, and obedience, they are not sensitive. They do not quickly respond to the whispered suggestions of conscience, nor to the gentle influence of the indwelling Holy Spirit. Hence they give a sort of slovenly service to God—the kind of worship that befits dullards, not soaring spirits.

To be sure, God does make occasional use of extraordinary departures from His common laws, sometimes for a hidden purpose of His own, sometimes for reasons that are obvious even to us. But to the faithful disciple, all the dispensations of His providence are acceptable, whether ordinary or extraordinary; for He is both perfectly good and absolutely omnipotent.

If my will is right, it automatically accords with God's. What He chooses, I choose. Even if I should feel that an exception is desirable, and therefore, in childlike fashion, should present my petition for a miracle, I shall submit my request only as a tentative wish, subject to God's approval. Moreover—and this is important—I must not be habitually on the lookout for wonders and predisposed to find them where they do not exist. The kind of faith which Jesus inculcates is content with God as He is, and with the world as He made it. His most loyal disciples see Him and find Him good, in every time, and in every place, and in every set of circumstances. I wish to be like that; and I will try!

3rd WEEK AFTER EPIPHANY
PROVISIONAL MEDITATION—TUESDAY
Be Thou Made Clean (Matt. 8, 3)

GOD IS not limited by the order of nature which He Himself established. He can suspend natural laws; many times He has suspended them. We believe this quite readily. I should have but a foolish idea of God, if I did not attribute omnipotence to Him. And my faith in Your divinity, dear Lord, implies my faith in Your omnipotence. Your miracles proved this to those who saw You with bodily eyes; but, with no need of any such proof, I acknowledge You as my Lord and my God.

In the life of the soul, God often acts as He did with the lepers to whom He said, "Be thou made clean." Indeed, if it were not that the word "miracle" is properly applied only to rare, exceptional occurrences, the forgiveness of sins in confession would be called a miracle; it is a greater wonder than the healing of leprosy. No matter what we call it, the cure of spiritual illness is a marvelous deed; and what joy there is in the thought that Christians live on a high level where supernatural favors of one kind or another are bestowed in practically uninterrupted succession from the beginning to the end of life.

Each one of us has reason to feel as the grateful leper felt. In my own case, no protestation of gratitude can be too enthusiastic; for no words could possibly express my appreciation of what God has done. Wonders multiplied before my eyes each day would hardly deepen my faith; I know that unseen miracles of forgiveness have been worked in my own soul, over and over again. With this in mind, I shall, I hope, not ever be strongly tempted to be impatient with what I do not understand in God's dispensations. When I ask for His favors, I know that He will give me whatever I need, and at the time I need it; and I pledge myself now to accept His choice, His time, His method. Therefore, I move through the world content—sure of His wisdom and His goodness when I do not see His plan; ever grateful and trustful, even when there is no visible evidence that He is aware of my suffering and my needs.

181

I Will Come and Cure Him (Matt. 8, 7)

WHATEVER God promises is as good as done. So the centurion thought. So the saint thinks. So should we think. Always and in all circumstances God keeps His word. There may be physical obstacles in the way; there may be natural laws involved; we may have no evidence that God is about to do as He promised, in fact, all the appearances may be quite to the contrary. Nevertheless, we are positively, absolutely, immovably sure that what He has promised, this He will accomplish—if we fulfill the conditions He has laid down. What He promises is as good as done.

How great a relief to anxious minds would be this quiet, Christian confidence! To be sure, troubles and dangers may intervene. We may have to wait for a while, or even to suffer. But a man's real anxiety, deepest care, trouble, concern, worry, revolves around the final, permanent result of his striving. If he is sure of the ultimate attainment of the desirable end, then all intervening labor and pain and failure are minimized. And it is precisely with regard to the ultimate result, that the Christian has God's assurance. *In te Domine speravi!* In Thee, O Lord, have I hoped! I shall not be abandoned.

In view of all this, a faithful disciple of Jesus is at peace deep down in his soul—no matter how great the superficial disturbance of his daily life may be. He has no real worry; because he has no doubt as to the eventual future. We cannot forecast tomorrow's evils. The price of following in Our Master's footsteps is high; the path is steep; the cross is heavy. Gethsemane and Calvary are dark, forbidding prospects. Yet finally all will be well. And, although we know little about next week or next year, we know all about the Last Day. As with St. Teresa, nothing can disturb us, nothing affright us, because to those who love God, the end of life will usher in a perpetual Epiphany in Heaven!

3rd WEEK AFTER EPIPHANY
PROVISIONAL MEDITATION—THURSDAY
Does This Scandalize You? (John 6, 62)

THESE words were addressed to the disciples after Jesus had become aware that some of them were complaining over His "strange talk" about eating His flesh and drinking His blood. To those of His followers who were on the point of leaving Him, He addressed the challenging question: "Does this scandalize you?" We may imagine that Our Lord puts the same question to those who find His ways with men difficult to understand—to every young idealist, now weaned and almost ready to falter; to the self-sacrificing, whose savings are being wasted by the self-indulgent; to the charitable, whose open door is crowded with lazy imposters; to the believer, whose faith is derided by the disillusioned and the cynical; to the honest truthteller, who is mocked as a fool; to every servant of faith and hope and love, who is tempted to accept the viewpoint of the world.

It should surprise no disciple to find the sayings of Jesus hard, to see that the path to Heaven is narrow and rough. Yet whenever virtue, even heroic virtue, goes unrewarded, the most loyal heart is disposed to sink. Doubt may present itself: "Are my sacrifices worth while?" At such a moment one needs to remember the divine origin of those ideals which Jesus revealed to the world—and also the record of their actual efficacy in the transformation of mankind. The cross, sometimes frightening when seen so close, becomes in perspective the symbol of salvation. Where would humanity be but for the cross? Where should I be? And how could the Christian saint ever have been shaped and fashioned without the cross?

Since that day when the disciples turned away because of the hard saying uttered by Jesus, many fainthearted followers of His have abandoned Him. Let me never do this. To me He has spoken plainly. He has warned me of the hardships involved in following the path He trod. I see that I must either accept the cross or abandon Him. I choose the cross.

WHEN Jesus asked, "Do you also wish to go away?" Peter replied, "To whom shall we go?" It is the perfect answer. It implies the impossibility of finding any adequate substitute for Jesus. It implies that to leave Him is to lose everything desirable, to court disaster. It is a profession of wholehearted, intelligent, undying loyalty. Blessed be Peter, who thus provided us with a formula fit for use in every moment of temptation, who thus gave us an unanswerable argument against sin. For every temptation is reducible to an invitation to leave God; otherwise there would be no question of sin and no temptation.

There are temptations in which the invitation to abandon Jesus is cleverly hidden, glossed over, dimmed, muted. But there it is. Training and grace will enable us to pierce through the plausible appearances of words and circumstances, to go straight to the heart of the matter, to face the main issue, which is always this: "Shall I, or shall I not, turn away from Jesus?" The counter-question that makes all further discussion superfluous and absurd is to be found in Peter's answer. "To whom shall I go?" Thus with irresistible force the truth is driven into my conscience, that it must be Jesus or no one. I must be at His side, or nowhere. There is no further need of discussion, of dispute, of hesitation.

To You I go, dear Lord; with You I stay. Let me always see clearly who it is that invites me elsewhere and what it is that I am offered as an alternative to Your friendship. For he that invites is the evil one, and what he offers me is sin. If I leave Your side, even for a moment, I may go completely astray and lose You forever. Therefore, I am resolved to grasp Your hand fast and never let it go. For "to be with You is paradise, and to be away from You is grievous torment."

He Who Does Not Believe Will Be Condemned
(Mark 16, 16)

FAITH IS an assent to what is said by one whom I trust. I believe, not because I can prove the truth to which I assent, but because I have confidence in the one who proposes the truth, that is to say, God. The believer need not be a scholar. The genius is not rated higher in the kingdom of God than the child. God is no more partial to scientists and philosophers than to the vast uncultured multitude.

Faith, being a virtue, implies the participation of the will. This makes clear what at first sight seems confusing, namely, that a man may be blamed and even punished for refusing to believe. The response of the men and the women to whom Christ addressed His message while upon earth was a measure of their appreciation of Him; and that appreciation was, in turn, an expression of their whole character. Many elements enter into a man's decision to accept and follow Christ. The making of this fateful decision may be described as the culmination of one's whole previous life; for capacity to see the truth, readiness to do right, ability to sense values, depend upon one's habitual attitude toward the temptations that present one with a never ending series of chances to choose between good and evil. It is as if an unspoiled instinct were making the believer aware that a divine Being is speaking to him with the voice of the Man, Jesus Christ.

Jesus teaches that refusal to believe is not merely a misfortune, but a fault. My readiness to believe, my good will in responding to every presentation of truth that God makes to me, is affected by everything I have ever done up to the present time. Past actions have shaped and fashioned me into such form that I readily believe, or into such that I easily hesitate and reject. If I do not believe, it is my own fault, and I shall be condemned. Dear Lord, to the limit of my ability, I do now believe.

Do Not Be Afraid of Those Who Kill the Body
(Matt. 10, 28)

To FEAR a man—in the sense here used—puts one at his mercy. Moved by fear, I substitute his will for my own. Unless I have the courage to defy him, to face his wrath, he can force me to go his way, to shape my conduct, not according to my own preference, but according to his. To a normal individual, this subservience is intolerable. God has given me the gift of freedom, the power to choose for myself a way of life, a course of action. I do not willingly relinquish it.

Most frequently it is in the minor circumstances of life that I am called upon to control my fear of man. For most of us, it will not be a question of resisting physical violence, not a matter of torture or death; but rather of holding fast to a principle disliked by those around us, or of doing something unpopular at a particular time or place. Occasionally, however, we must be prepared to resist compulsion even at the risk of suffering violence or death itself. Among those who can kill the body, Our Lord no doubt includes all who are in a position to put pressure on us in order to make us act against our consciences. These we are never to obey. We are to follow the path God points out—follow it at any cost. We are to cherish our divine ideals; and we are not to fear.

The martyrs feared nothing and nobody. Nothing and nobody could deter them from obedience to God, from following the promptings of conscience. In every walk of life they appear; in every imaginable set of circumstances, they are dauntless and unafraid. O Blessed Martyrs, how much I owe to you! How strongly I am encouraged by your example! May I at least in some small degree resemble you!

4th WEEK AFTER EPIPHANY
PROVISIONAL MEDITATION—MONDAY
Why Are You Fearful? (Matt. 8, 26)

THERE is a lesson for all of us in the reproach addressed by Jesus to the disciples terrified at the storm, while He slept near them, apparently unaware of the danger. His words imply that their fright was unjustified and consequently discreditable; and the lesson He taught applies to most of us. We become fearful because we have not fixed our attention on the proper object. The attitude of the blessed in Heaven may serve us as a model; their attention is fixed on the divine Presence. Similar to this is the attitude of the saint here upon earth, whose absorbed attention to God is matched by his brave indifference to matters which frighten lesser men. If we are like the blessed in Heaven or like the saint, we shall be free from fear.

What keeps me fretted with worry, tense and anxious about what may happen? My excessive self-consciousness. I keep looking at my prospects of profit or loss, my chance of winning or losing comfort and luxury and friends and income and security. With my attention thus wrongly focused and my will improperly directed, of course my world is all out of proportion; and inevitably its disorder affects me.

What then should I do? I should establish a habit of control over my thoughts. I shall be able to do this, if I devote only a minor portion of my attention to self, and center my mind upon God. The disciples in the boat apparently were thinking about themselves when they should have been thinking about Jesus. He would have them serene with the serenity that comes from faith. I must then practice attention to the ever-present God, total abandonment to His Will. As fear is a symptom of mental and moral weakness, so unshaken confidence in divine Providence is a good sign of spiritual health.

BUT FOR Our Lord Jesus Christ, every one of us would have good reason to fear dreadful things; for it is by Him and by Him alone, that we are freed from the power of sin. He it is who opens the gates of Heaven to us. No man comes to the Father save through Him. Now, however, we are indeed sure of salvation if we are one with Him in mind and will. To live as far as possible in His Presence, then, to study His teaching and imitate His behavior will exclude all reasons for fear. If we are following Him wholeheartedly, we are in no danger of hell, because we are in no danger of offending the heavenly Father.

To see Christ here and now, day by day, hour by hour; to speak to Him in childlike fashion; to think out carefully what He Himself would do or say in our circumstances is effectively to put ourselves under His influence. This is the way to get rid of fear; because this is the way to forestall the possibility of offending God. On the other hand, if we are not doing our best to be like Him, we should indeed be fearful.

The difficulties which confront me and the temptations which assail me need give me no alarm, if I am in His Presence. Nerves may for the moment be disturbed; my heart may quake at the sight and the thought of obstacles too great for me to overcome. Yet faith tells me plainly that His grace gives me strength to do whatever I am really obliged to do. My best will always be sufficient for God; but it has to be my best—nothing less. At times I am prone to worry over problems that are unanswerable. If unanswerable, they do not need to be answered. It would be wiser to focus my attention and effort on the one thing needful, the one indispensable object—namely, correspondence with grace; harmony of my will with God's Will; trying honestly to see His purpose and to fulfill it.

Be Afraid of Him Who Is Able to Destroy Both Soul and Body (Matt. 10, 28)

MUCH foolishness has been spoken and written with regard to fear. We are told "to fear nothing." This advice is silly and dangerous to follow. There are many things that should be feared—God's displeasure most of all. There is a sane and proper fear of God which is related to sin and sin's punishment. Were there no sin and no punishment of sin, there would be no room for this fear. But it is blind folly for the sinner not to fear; and it is wholly irrational. Why not fear God? Why not seek to satisfy His outraged justice by sorrow, by amendment, by penance, before death comes? That is a question to which no one can find a satisfactory answer. A sinner who does not fear is suffering one of the most appalling consequences of sin—blindness, hardheartedness. He is out of touch with reality. He plunges to his fate like a maniac, a madman. Dreadful state of soul, this. Yet not uncommon.

Fear is literally the beginning of wisdom; it is a prerequisite of rational conduct; it is indispensable to a virtuous life. In every reasonable being, fear is closely allied to sorrow and to the purpose of amendment. Thus it often happens that fear becomes the initial motive for a soul that has been selfish to accept the proffered aid of God and correspond with the first grace. Here we have one good reason for the custom of preaching mission sermons on everlasting punishment, and for meditations on hell.

To disobey God without fear is, of course, equivalent to despising Him—a procedure as unreasonable as that of the man who swallows carbolic acid, or jumps into a blazing furnace. It would be wiser to wrestle with a wild tiger or grasp a high tension wire than to despise God. Grant me the gift of holy fear, dear Lord. May I be stricken with terror at the very prospect of offending You!

Seek First the Kingdom of God and His Justice
Matt. 6, 33)

IT IS a bad mistake for a man to concentrate attention and effort upon the lesser at the expense of the greater. Yet ordinary human nature is inclined to do precisely this, and thereby to fall into no end of trouble, both material and spiritual. The text warns us to seek first things first; and it reminds us of Our Lord's challenging question, "What does it profit a man, if he gains the whole world, but suffer the loss of his own soul?"

We are not to interpret the text as a promise that the disciples of Jesus will grow rich. The hundredfold reward applies to finer quality rather than to more quantity. The disciple will receive something far more precious than the bauble which tempts him, something unspeakably better than the thing on which the worldling spends his effort. We are always better off when we refuse to turn away from the narrow path which leads to the kingdom of God.

If the artist seeks money or popularity, he loses his best chance of reaching the peak of perfection. It is when he is striving, as it were impersonally, to express truth and beauty that he comes nearest to creating a perfect work, timeless and irresistible. So, too, an athlete will reach his highest level when he concentrates upon his effort, as if he were indifferent to praise or prizes. All of us, without being artists or athletes, can readily perceive the value of putting "first things first"; for, in one way or another, it is exemplified in all our lives. Most impressively does this truth stand out in the activity of the saint, who seeks first the kingdom of God and yet misses nothing worth the having. Let me make the application of this same principle to my own life.

Do Not Be Anxious . . . for Your Body (Matt. 6, 25)

THIS prohibition of Our Lord does not forbid reasonable attention to physical health. But it does bar us from giving a disproportionate amount of time to the body and thus disturbing peace of soul. In the first place physical interests never deserve as much attention as spiritual welfare; so that one who neglects the soul for sake of the body is necessarily and always at fault. Moreover, no matter how much trouble we take, we can never be perfectly sure of safeguarding our physical well-being; and, if we allow ourselves to be too much concerned about it, we run the risk of losing both substance and shadow and of wrecking both the present and the future.

We are not, of course, to assume that it will never cost us anything to do the Will of God. It is only a distorted Gospel that invites men to believe they will always be materially better off, if they devote themselves primarily to the things of the spirit and put material and bodily interests in the second place. Jesus gives no such guarantee. The men and women who take Him at His word have often suffered much. They have gone hungry; they have been clothed in rough garments; they have been poorly sheltered. They have suffered from lack of sufficient sleep. Despite all this, however, they abound in spiritual wealth; and they are the most fortunate and the most joyous of men.

The consoling point of Christ's teaching is that His followers are free from profound worry and anxiety. No real evil can happen to the disciple who, caring little for himself, is cared for, in the truest sense, by God. All things work together for his good; and whatever he has foregone on earth for the Master's sake, will be returned to him multiplied and supernaturalized in the kingdom of Heaven. Please God, I shall build my life upon this truth and never forget it, never doubt it.

4th WEEK AFTER EPIPHANY
PROVISIONAL MEDITATION—SATURDAY

Which of You by Being Anxious . . . Can Add to Stature? (Matt. 6, 27)

IT IS a mark of a good general to know when to retreat. A wise man stops at the proper time and place. Not to know when to stop is typical of the obsessed man, the fanatic. To spend time and strength on plans that are literally impossible is pure waste.

Our Lord's disciples are taught to restrain their desires within reasonable and lawful limits; they devote time and attention to things that can be done and should be done. If they dream dreams, it is to some good purpose. Their visions have an influence, a resonance in actual life. They direct their energies not toward impracticable, imaginary, fantastic aims, but to the realizing of high, noble, holy deeds. They begin with learning the art of self-denial. Thus they are able to channel thought and energy; with them there is no waste motion, no lost time. Examining the life of a saint, or even a day of that life, we perceive that the saint is taken up exclusively with the planning and executing of God's holy Will. He does not spend himself in wishing things were otherwise; or in lamenting the difficult curcumstances in which God's Providence has placed him; or in postponing effort until some future time and some not yet realized set of circumstances. He is not dreaming of adding a cubit to his stature by thinking about it. Being a saint, he is realistic. The saints are always precisely that.

In the text, Our Lord instructs us to be practical. He draws attention to the fact that there is a certain sphere into which we need not and cannot enter, because it is the province of God. Let me take this recommendation to heart. Recognizing the limitations imposed upon me by the laws of nature and by the Will of God, let me devote my time and attention to aims that are both attainable and spiritually profitable.

Let Both Grow Until the Harvest (Matt. 13, 30)

GOD'S WAYS are not our ways. Hence, when God does or leaves undone certain things—when, for example, He lets the good suffer, while the evil prosper—we may be tempted to impatience, or resentment, or even doubt. The parable of the sower is therefore helpful. Just as a superficial observer may think it silly of the farmer to let weeds grow in his field, a shortsighted Christian may begin to doubt God's goodness and wisdom, if those attributes are hidden under misleading appearances. But God is never at fault. He cannot be.

The parable suggests that behind puzzling actions and policies, there may be good reasons which we cannot see. It does not follow that two different courses of conduct are really irreconcilable with each other, just because I do not know how to reconcile them. A thousand difficulties do not make one doubt. God is never less than infinitely loving and perfectly just—otherwise He would not be God. He may be tolerating undesirable conditions because to end them would be the occasion of introducing a greater evil.

"The mills of God grind slowly." It is not for us to fix the time when the wicked shall be called to account and justice done. That old proverb, "the best is the enemy of the good," means that a man bent on making things perfect may do more harm than good in his well meant attempt. There is much egotism in the impatient zeal which insists upon rooting up weeds, even at the cost of injuring the wheat. It is somtimes one of "the lingering imperfections of the saints." Be never impatient with God, then, O my soul! Never doubt Him. If He refrains from intervening in situations that dismay and terrify, trust His goodness and His love.

Blessed Art the Poor in Spirit (Matt. 5, 3)

FROM THE moment of our birth, the material world exerts influence upon us. As we open our eyes wider and wider, it becomes more attractive, more alluring. It promises to satisfy our desires, to still urges that persistently disturb us, to allay deep longings that brook no refusal. Comfort beckons; curiosity impels us to explore; beauty dazzles; power intoxicates; money—symbol and pledge of wealth—deludes us with its promise of present satisfaction and of permanent rest from labor and trouble. But all these promises are deceitful. If we trust them, we are lost. I must never forget that my spiritual existence depends upon my remembering that material things are not what they seem.

As time goes on, we meet pleasures that attract us and we feel inner desires that urge us. This combination can be resisted only by a combination of well developed habits and God's powerful grace. Conspicuous among those habits is poverty of spirit—an outstanding characteristic of Christ and of all His disciples. Who could imagine a luxury-loving, self-indulgent, hardship-hating saint? When the habit of poverty has overcome the alliance of inner appetite and outer excitement, then and then only we shall be free, detached, able to move about in the visible world almost like disembodied spirits, who are never held down, nor cramped by material things.

Let me examine myself, to see if I have attained the freedom which comes with poverty. Is there anything to which I still cling unreasonably, inordinately? If so, I must renounce it, in order to possess that quality which enables the soul to triumph over natural human attachments. "Blessed are the poor in spirit!" Give me this blessing, dear Lord. Help me to make myself poor. Compel me to renounce.

IF POVERTY comes first in the transformation of a worldling into a Christian, meekness comes second. After having given up outer things, one goes on to the renunciation of self. Poverty and meekness are like outer and inner aspects of the same virtue. Or we may say that meekness perfects what poverty has begun. For only when a man by meekness has divested himself of egotism, does his will harmonize perfectly with the Will of the heavenly Father.

Meekness checks the instinct to attach undue importance to self—the instinct which gets us off center, out of tune, away from the line marked out by God. Meekness, checking that instinct, controls egotism; it adjusts us to God; it puts us in our proper place with regard to the whole created universe. It enables us to share in the life of God; for in the measure that we are emptied of self we are filled with Him. In one word, meekness is our passport to the kingdom of Heaven.

We must not, however, make the mistake of confusing meekness with softness. The meek show a stubborn, and sometimes unexpected, resistance when worldlings wish to make them substitute social conventions for supernatural ideals. Unlike the worldling, the meek soul assumes that the laws of the kingdom of Heaven are not less, but more, powerful than the physical laws which rule the universe; that spiritual ideals are not less, but more, real than the forces which enter into the calculations of the chemist and the engineer. Every truth imparted to us by our great Teacher, Jesus, is like a constant in a mathematical problem. It never changes. It must always be taken into our calculations. The power of self-love, irresistible on the natural level, must ever be counterbalanced by meekness. Jesus is meek. The saints are meek. Am I?

By Your Patience You Will Win Your Souls
(Luke 21, 19)

THE WISE man always esteems the heroic quality of patience. And when a man who has been outrageously abused keeps his temper, even the crowd applauds. How edified we are when disappointment is accepted smilingly, when pain is borne without complaint. Only seasoned troops stand still under fire. The test of a fighter's quality is his ability to "take it." Runners tell us that the hardest thing in a race is to hold back until the moment comes for the winning spurt.

Life tests all of us. The young, if true to type, are over-eager for action, inclined to spoil things by plunging forward. Older people find it hard to be patient, because they are less elastic, less resilient than the young; and time is slipping. Persons in ill health often acquire a habit of impatience, taking advantage of the fact that they can do this with impunity. Yet in youth and in age, in temptation and in affliction, all of us must practice patience. Otherwise we shall not resemble Jesus, who praises this virtue so highly, or the saints whose patience is proverbial—"patient as a saint."

All of us can—indeed, we must—train ourselves to endure silently and cheerfully the unpleasant experiences of daily life. We can, for example, keep ourslves from thinking of irritating persons and depressing facts. We can abstain from talking about these things; we can focus attention on something else. We thus acquire a certain degree of immunity from the virus of impatience; we thus make life smoother, both for ourselves and our neighbors. The humble virtue of patience, so hard to acquire, brings something of that calm peace which makes life in Heaven different from life on earth. Also —what is much more important—it pleases God, whose joy in the patient man is so vividly described in the Book of Job. God, grant me patience!

Blessed Are They Who Mourn (Matt. 5, 5)

CHRIST IS surely no enemy of joy. He brought peace into the world. He made eternal happiness possible. His religion is a source of cheer, not of sadness and gloom. Yet He recognizes—and His disciples must always recognize—the sad fact of human sin and human suffering. We are unlike Him, if we are indifferent to our fellow creature's pain, if we are unmoved so long as we ourselves remain untouched. A nature warped like that is out of sympathy with God and with man.

Without question, the most sensitive of all hearts is the Heart of Jesus; and especially is He sensitive to suffering. To all who lie under the blight of pain or shame, His loving sympathy goes out. His readiness to mourn with those who mourn is so far beyond my own that I cannot even get an adequate idea of it. Yet I do understand that in the sorrow of mankind—which is also His sorrow—I should, at least to some extent, participate. "Blessed are they who mourn."

I must then grieve not only over my own sins, but over the sins of the whole world. I must have sympathy with all human ills, never letting myself grow callous to the hideous sufferings that vast numbers of men and women are undergoing every day. To be sure, discomfort will come to me at remembrance of the pain that afflicts my neighbors; but I must not try to escape that discomfort. And for every one in sorrow and pain, I must pray, hoping that by God's grace and in God's way relief will come to them. Meanwhile, as a reinforcement of my prayer, I may well offer in their behalf the merits of all the suffering which I myself am bearing willingly and cheerfully for the love of God.

5th WEEK AFTER EPIPHANY
PROVISIONAL MEDITATION—FRIDAY
Blessed Are the Merciful (Matt. 5, 7)

PITY IS instinctive in noble souls. They are moved to sadness just because others are unhappy; they wish to give aid and consolation. This feeling is the very opposite of envy—that detestable inclination to grow sad at the sight of others possessing and enjoying what we ourselves lack. Raised to a high level by grace, pity becomes a beatitude. Those who mourn because others are mourning, readily become servants of the poor, and teachers of the ignorant, and missionaries in foreign lands. They give generously of their time, their energy, their material resources to the helpless, the delinquent, the submerged.

Souls that experience sadness at the misfortune of others turn to the practice of penance as a matter of course. Not only do they see the peculiar value of mortification as an instrument of self-discipline, as a means of making the soul Christlike; but they also discover in it a sort of mystical power to bind the children of God to one another in a helpful relationship. It is as if the pain of the helpless is somehow made less awful by the pain which their more fortunate neighbors freely choose and patiently endure.

This attitude of pity would seem to explain, at least in part, the saint's reluctance to dwell in comfort, his preference for hardship. It may become also to me a motive for accepting and prizing unpleasant things— even perhaps for seeking them. The subtle, invisible relationship of suffering and holiness—which are not obviously dependent upon each other—is something that every student of the saint discovers. Meditating on life, I soon learn that the rich and honored and pampered and luxurious and comfortable and carefree, those who wear fine linen and dwell in the houses of kings, are not so blessed as the merciful. And, therefore, I will abound in mercy. I will deny it to no one—to no one at all.

Blessed Are They Who Suffer Persecution for Justice' Sake (Matt. 5, 10)

THERE IS much talk about justice. But few are loyal to its demands, if those demands run counter to self-interest. When they threaten our comfort, or property, when they involve loss of popular esteem and perhaps even seem to invite persecution, then most of us take cover. We turn a blind eye to the unjust deed that brings profit to us. We deny the truth that is discreditable to ourselves or harmful to our interests. We employ different standards in judging the conduct of friends and of enemies. We ignore the demands of fair play; and we favor our associates against other groups, social, racial, or religious.

These things are incompatible with loyalty to Jesus. If we are truly His disciples, we must judge just judgment, holding the individual innocent until proven guilty, resisting all pressure from within or without. I should be the friend of the weak, the sinful, the stranger, the alien. If, in so doing, I bring hardships upon myself, then I shall be suffering persecution for justice' sake.

I greatly fear that I am far from ready to suffer even the lightest sort of persecution for justice' sake. I have been deterred from following my conscience, or keeping my resolution, by obstacles so petty as to seem ridiculous when I look back at them—a sneer from someone, or a pitying smile, or an unexpected experience of discomfort. Not of such stuff are saints made. There must be at least a little heroism in one who undertakes to follow Christ. Not for nothing do we honor the martyrs and bear their names. Persecution for justice' sake can never harm me. Let me keep this well in mind. Persecution patiently endured will make me blessed. Our Lord has said so. I must never doubt it. And I must prove my faith in Him, my loyalty to His principles, no matter what others say or do, no matter what sort of persecution I may suffer.

The Kingdom of Heaven Is Like a Grain of Mustard Seed (Matt. 13, 31)

THE PARABLE of the mustard seed suggests many thoughts to many minds. One of the truths it illustrates is that Christ established a new scale of values for His disciples. Those who are last in the world are first in the kingdom of God; the greatest become the least. This is a comforting thought; for most of us must make our way toward Heaven not by deeds that attract notice, not by heroic achievements, but by sorrow for sin, by doing penance, by loyal obedience to God in the practice of humble virtues. Through the grace of God, what was of itself merely a weak human effort acquires divine value. Man, co-operating with grace, takes on the very image and likeness of his Maker.

Our petty daily duties, then, like the little mustard seed, possess amazing potency. They have a merit which does not necessarily attach to the achievements of a genius or a hero, no matter how highly men may esteem these latter. For the Creator of the physical universe is also the Creator of moral values. And the ultimate worth of everything is determined by the rating He gives it.

As I go about my ordinary routine, I should bear all this in mind. The remembrance of the mustard seed will shine like a light in dark places. It will help to nullify the depression that attends misfortune and failure. For superficial things pass away; whereas, out of simple deeds, God builds up a kingdom infinitely greater than all other kingdoms—one that shall never pass. Let me then this day resolve just to do my duty. Let me build slowly, stone upon stone, beam joined to beam. Let me build carefully; for this is a house for God that I am constructing. Let me build gratefully; for in this house I shall dwell with Him forever!

Bring in . . . the Poor, and the Crippled, and the Blind, and the Lame (Luke 14, 21)

ONE MAY discover much about a man by observing his attitude toward underprivileged, helpless persons. Most of us would violently resent the charge, or even the suspicion, of having oppressed the weak; we dislike all bullies. Yet bullying is really not uncommon. How often an official, a master, a teacher, a parent abuses authority by taking advantage of those who are unable to resist—making shallow excuses for this sort of conduct. How often they rationalize their behavior —alleging imaginary good motives, instead of acknowledging the actual motives which are selfish and bad.

Those of us who possess power are subject to a subtle form of temptation which makes us to some extent like persons, dazzled, or delirious, or intoxicated. We do not see things as they really are. We regard principles and ideals as plastic forms that can be altered and modified according to circumstances. We place ourselves in the center of a small stage which looks to us like the universe. We get far away from distasteful realities. We forget that the moral law is immutable, that the poor have inalienable rights, that there is a divine court which decrees severe punishment for all who oppress the weak.

Instead of reflecting on the disturbing fact that few persons except the saints practice these fundamental Christian principles in their daily lives, I had better focus attention on my own individual shortcomings. The truth is that self-love continually influences me to discriminate in my own favor. My deeds, words, thoughts, plans, my very dreams, disclose me to be an unbalanced egotist. It would be a good beginning of improvement, were I to make myself act kindly and speak graciously to everyone without exception—paying special attention to persons who are under-privileged and most special attention to those who, for any reason, are distasteful to me.

Blessed Are the Peacemakers (Matt. 5, 9)

A SITUATION that threatens peace brings out the best qualities in some persons. Men who love peace will go far, work hard, give much to preserve it. With a kindly smile, a soothing word, ingenious effort, they manage to resolve, or to postpone, a crisis. It is impossible to foretell to what disastrous consequences a breach of peace may lead—violence, hatred, injustice, great suffering, lifelong estrangement. But against whatever evils may threaten, the peacemaker employs all his resources—a blessed task for which he will receive a rich reward.

The title of peacemaker belongs also—most emphatically—to the man who will not give back blow for blow, the man whose gentle answer abates anger and softens an adversary. It may be that to remain peaceful under provocation, will require a very great act of self-restraint. In proportion to the effort will be the blessing—or rather the blessing will be a thousand times as great.

One of the notorious paradoxes of modern life is this, that wars are usually declared by persons who do not fight in them. So, too, on the smaller battlefields of personal quarrels, trouble is often provoked by a third party —a talebearer, a gossiper, a disturbing spirit, one who is the antithesis of a peacemaker and who merits therefore not reward but punishment. Whether the issue be great or small, let me align myself with the peacemakers and follow their principles loyally. How fine a thing to go about among friends and acquaintances, touching everything and everybody with the olive branch of peace, spreading never dissension but always better understanding. This may imply much self-restraint; it may require great generosity; it may bring upon me at times sharp criticism. All that would be a small price to pay; for the sure reward is very great—the blessing of the peacemaker.

Blessed Are the Clean of Heart (Matt. 5, 8)

PURE-HEARTEDNESS is much more comprehensive than chastity. It concerns not only the body, but heart and mind and one's whole nature. "Pure" means free from alloy, untainted, stainless, perfect. Purity of heart is a phrase favored by spiritual teachers—Father Lallemant for example—who tells us that it implies wholehearted, unreserved consecration to the Will of God. Purity of heart excludes from the soul any opposition, however slight, to the working of divine grace. Pureheartedness, therefore, is not attained, until the disciple has cut off every encumbrance, renounced every association, terminated all reluctance and hesitation that interfere with his unconditioned and all-embracing surrender of self. The pure of heart belong to God, not only by reason of His sovereign claim upon their allegiance, but also by reason of their concurring, total giving-over of themselves.

It is clear, then, that to be pure of heart, one must have examined oneself long and carefully, one must have arrived at a true diagnosis of one's spiritual maladies. In other words, we make progress toward purity of heart by recognizing at last the true character of certain favorite false notions we have cherished; by setting in order old, perverse tendencies which have distorted the pattern of conduct designed for us by God. Muddy water must be cleansed; the blood must be purified of infection; the whole organism must be revivified. All this implies that we shall co-operate satisfactorily with divine grace only when we make the best possible use of our natural faculties.

On the basis of the considerations just reviewed, I begin to realize why purity of heart is a prerequisite for the vision of God; and I see that purity is a mighty task which will require all my time and all my energy. I can afford to waste nothing; for I shall see God, only if I am pure of heart—not otherwise. Give me purity, dear Lord; and give it to me now.

They . . . Are as Angels in Heaven (Mark 12, 25)

CHASTITY is known as "the angelic virtue." The word "chastity" is often used interchangeably with the word "purity." Perhaps the reason for this is that sex lies at the very roots of life—it is the powerful instinct on which the race depends for existence. The attainment of perfect chastity is thus closely associated with that complete triumph over the lower self which we call "purity of heart." But the two are not identical.

Chastity makes us angelic; not because the chaste are free from temptation; not because they can ignore the subtle snares of passion; but because, by reason of constant vigilance, habitual self-discipline, abundant grace, they have attained serenity—like the strong man who imposes peace by force of arms. It is instructive to recall that Saint Benedict and Saint Francis wrestled with temptation and that David and Solomon fell.

The knowledge of human nature which we gain, either by struggling with our own temptations or by observing the conduct of others, makes plain the intimate relationship between faith and chastity. The connection between impurity and blindness is not so difficult to understand, when we recall the fact that sensual indulgence enfeebles the soul. It is the simple, the pure of heart, who see God. It is the simple, the pure of heart, who attain chastity. They possess that clear vision which is characteristic of penitent souls; that unquestioning conformity to the Will of God which involves heroic renunciation. Cleansed by penance, strengthened by recurrent struggles with temptations, one is enlinghtened and inspired by the sense of God's Presence and the inflowing of His grace—one walks in the shadow of the valley of death, unharmed. Give me chastity, then, dear Lord. And give me this precious gift quickly.

Go and Do Thou Also in Like Manner (Luke 10, 37)

THESE words point the moral of the Good Samaritan parable. They should remind us first of all of the essential unity of the human race. For mankind is one, with a unity that transcends every superficial difference of distance, or class, or nation, or race. No barriers cut off the children of God from one another. As they are all members of the same family, the resources of the earth belong to all; and all should share them. Each man has a right to his just portion. Such division as may be made, should be in the interests of the whole family. Any method of distribution which injures the common good is, on that account, illegal and invalid.

Yet who will deny that the lesson taught by Jesus nineteen centuries ago is still unlearned? Some of us hoard, while others starve. Some of us indulge in luxury, while others lack necessities. We withhold and appropriate more than our share — as if the beggar and vagrant had not a divinely-given, inalienable right to as much as befits a man; as if his title were not as valid as ours, no matter what our title may be. Thus we equivalently deny that the spirit of poverty is an integral element of the Christian character.

Let me practice poverty, then, not by giving gifts to the poor, with the condescension of a king bestowing favors upon his subjects or of a master rewarding his servants, but rather as an heir of a family estate, or a partner in an enterprise, undertaking to divide equitably what has come into his hands. To do this, presupposes a divine ideal, the unselfish ideal of the homeless, penniless Jesus; but thus and thus only can I resemble Him. And to resemble Him is my fondest hope, my dearest dream. Dear Lord, make it come true!

Freely You Have Received, Freely Give (Matt. 10, 8)

IT IS GOOD from time to time to enumerate the gifts we have received from God. How many they are! How wonderful! How deeply in His debt are we! Now persons hopelessly in debt, and without prospects of ever discharging their obligations, should be humble. Humility then, befits all of us; since we are indebted to God for literally everything that we have and even everything that we are. Here also is a compelling motive to give to others lavishly. Creditors are supposed to be exacting and hard—but not debtors. A debtor should be kindly, generous. And I am a debtor, not a creditor; because I am able to give nothing that is really mine. I can give only what God has loaned me in order that I may give it away again.

The disciples of Jesus are characteristically generous. They, of all men, are most ready to give until it hurts. A feature of our self-training, therefore, must be constant exercise in generous giving. We have little to give perhaps; but everyone has time—if not much, at least a little. And time is something we must give freely to God and, for His sake, to our neighbor. Jesus gave long hours to the worship of His heavenly Father; and He gave the rest of His time to the service of mankind. The saints did likewise. This is what I must try to do.

As every moment is precious, I am enormously rich. Nevertheless, if I am extravagant and wasteful, even my store of millions of precious moments will eventually run out; and I shall have no more time. Let me give time, while I have it, to the worship of God, to deeds of kindness toward my neighbor. Freely I have received, let me freely give. Again and again I tell myself I am a debtor, a debtor, a debtor. Therefore I must give, give, give.

24th (and Last) WEEK AFTER PENTECOST—SUNDAY

My Time Is Near (Matt. 26, 18)

THE GOSPEL of the last Sunday after Pentecost fore-tells the destruction of Jerusalem which ended an era of religious history. This Gospel also describes the chaos which will immediately precede the second coming of the Son of Man, and the last judgment. In our country the closing weeks of the Liturgical Year coincide with autumn which registers nature's passing from the summer of life to the winter of death. These things bring home the truth that for each one of us, young or old, time is running out. We share the feelings of the poet, looking at the autumn fields, who felt tears "rise in the heart and gather to the eyes"; or of the aviator who, plummeting to a fatal crash, whispers to himself, awe-stricken, "This is death!"

Fittingly, then, toward the end of the Liturgical Year, we turn our thoughts to the transient nature of the universe. By contrast with it, we perceive that spiritual realities are everlasting: the soul and the moral values it has created; the merit acquired with the help of God's grace; the kind words, generous deeds, acts of adoration and human service wrought under the influence of Christ's example. These are the realities that ripple out on the shoreless ocean of eternity—they last forever. After the glowing sun and the shining stars have crumpled into nothingness, neither God nor the soul will perish; nor will the good that His servants do ever pass away.

And so, dear Lord, in the words of an old Carthusian, I say to You, "O Defender and Consoler, protect and free us from all temptations and violence; console us with holy hope, and confidence, and the sweetness of love. As we depart this life, receive us and purge us; and, when we are cleansed, beatify us with the sight of You forever!"

207

24th (and Last) WEEK AFTER PENTECOST— MONDAY

They Do Not Know Him Who Sent Me (John 15, 21)

A MONG THE destructive tendencies that threaten society is diminishing knowledge of God. In order to measure the spread of this ignorance, we should take into account the fact that many who use His name— even though they use it with superficial reverence—do not really believe in His omnipotence. For practical use they have fashioned the idea of a God with whom they themselves are on a level of equality, a God who is their "partner" and is to some extent dependent on them.

Now the recognition of the infinity of God is of the very essence of true religion—the keystone of the arch. Without a conviction of His infinity, adoration is an impossibility, a contradiction of terms. Not only in our mental life, but also in our moral conduct, this conviction plays an irreplaceable part. The will, like the mind, must be adjusted to the infinite One. Human claims against God cannot exist; our dependence is total; our obligation is unlimited. There are persons who, like the Pharisees of whom Our Lord spoke, remain spiritually stubborn, blind, deaf. It seems hard to believe that they themselves realize the extent of their perversity; yet they do persist in it perhaps for years.

Let me ask: Have I been zealous in winning souls to knowledge of the truth and to Your obedience, dear Lord? Have I been solicitous about Your honor which, in so many ways and in the minds of so many persons, is affected by my behavior? Have I always been careful to examine my motives in taking this side or that side of a disputed question? Have I exercised all my possible influence, defending the right and assailing the wrong? Or have I, through my obstinacy and selfishness and resentment and injustice, given others a wrong impression of Your ideals and of the divine truths You taught?

24th (and Last) WEEK AFTER PENTECOST—TUESDAY

Let Him Not Turn Back (Matt. 24, 18)

BEGINNINGS are difficult. A familiar proverb affirms, "It is the first step that costs." But, on the other hand, there are reasons for believing that it is not so difficult to begin as to persevere. Witness—if witness were needed—would be the perennial jest about New Year's resolutions. Everyone makes them; almost no one keeps them. Theologians give high rank to preseverance. Indeed they tell us that a special help of God is required, if we are to keep consistently free from fault even in the observance of the natural law.

One reason that we do not take a more serious view of our broken resolutions is that we do not realize how easily minor dislolayties may become major. When we yield to sloth; when we say to ourselves "For this time only"; when we dwell regretfully on dangerous occasions previously renounced; we are playing with fire, dancing on the edge of a precipice. Everyone knows how rigidly the vocalist, the acrobat, the aviator, must adhere to regulations necessary for muscular development and for the formation of helpful physical reactions. We must be no less eager than they to acquire habits that will make us fit to join the company of the saints.

Dear Lord, let me remember Your words, "No one having put his hand to the plow, and looking back, is fit for the kingdom of God." I see that worldlings, who are moved by selfish interests, obey their superiors much more faithfully than I obey You. They live up to the requirements of the schedule imposed on them. They consistently try to please the one from whom they expect to obtain a promotion. I am shamed by them; and I resolve to be more consistent, more presevering in the discharge of my spiritual duties. Grant, I beg of You, that every action of mine may commence under the inspiration of Your grace; and that, "once thus happily begun, it may also through You be happily ended."

Let Him Who Reads Understand (Matt. 24, 15)

AMONG interesting questions sometimes debated are these: "Do men ever hate the truth?" and "Is mental blindness a sin?" The answer is that, although men naturally love the truth, they often dislike it when they wish to be ignorant of a law that binds the conscience unpleasantly, or when they hope to circulate a false opinion of their merits. According to St. Thomas a man sins when he thus sets his selfish interests above his love of truth, when he shuts his eyes to facts in order to be free from moral restraint.

Most of us are ready to condemn a flat lie, the bearing of false witness, the falsifying of accounts; but loyalty to truth in minor matters is rather a rare quality—even among persons pledged to undertake spiritual progress. It is strangely inconsistent in us to seek opportunities for practicing voluntary mortification, while at the same time we are ready to equivocate or even to lie because the telling of the truth would involve a certain amount of discomfort or embarrassment. An early fruit of strict truth-telling is likely to be a divine strengthening of character. We grow as a result of criticism accepted from a neighbor, or made by ourselves.

Dear God, You have instructed the hearts of Your faithful by the light of the Holy Spirit. Grant us by the same Spirit always to relish the things that are right. May the outpouring of Your grace so cleanse and soften our hearts, that they may grow rich in good works. May my love of truth be stronger than all self-interest. Help me to tread the narrow path which leads to You, the everlasting Truth. I know that if I attempt to use all the light You send me, opportunities to suffer in the cause of truth will never be lacking. But of one thing I am sure, that to obey the summons of truth will mean that at long last I shall not regret it. For You never approve, and man never profits by, a lie.

24th (and Last) WEEK AFTER PENTECOST—
THURSDAY

They Shall See God (Matt. 5, 8)

IT IS A distorted concept of religion that gives the obligation of social service priority over the obligation of worship. To be sure, the Gospel insists upon our duty to love the neighbor as well as God; but to substitute the neighbor for God as our central interest would be to miss the purpose of the Gospel. Our Lord's message is dominated by the vision of the heavenly Father, more loving than earthly father or mother, who rewards good deeds a hundredfold, who watches over the ravens and the sparrows, and even over the lilies and the grass of the field. The aim of all Christ's teaching is to school His disciples in a steadily increasing consecration of mind and will, so that they may continually progress toward the bliss-bestowing, face-to-face vision of God in Heaven.

True religion, then, makes the worship of the heavenly Father the centerpiece, the cornerstone of our existence. We have been created to glorify God by adoring Him; and life on earth is truly profitable only insofar as it contributes to that union with God which will ultimately form the soul's everlasting happiness. The redeeming grace of Christ restores to man the power to rise from the contemplation of creatures to the contemplation of the Creator. In the souls of saints the exercise of this power lifts them up to a level, not only beyond the reach of lesser mortals but unintelligible to them. Self-discipline and social service predispose to, or result from, worship; they are always subordinate to the activity which focuses on the ever-present God.

For these lessons in the sacred science of the saints, we have You to thank, dear Lord. Beyond all power of expression is our obligation to give You honor. So once again, wholeheartedly I wish to pay tribute to You— You, the source of all that is really good and lovely and joy-bestowing in human life. Keep me from ever breaking this resolution, from ever doing You dishonor, my Lord and my God.

211

24th (and Last) WEEK AFTER PENTECOST— FRIDAY

Come, Blessed of My Father (Matt. 25, 34)

THE COMMUNION of saints presents us with the idea of a great family made up of the heavenly Father's children, some in Heaven, some in Heaven's ante-chamber, purgatory, some here upon earth. The title of saint belongs to all three classes—actually to the first, prospectively to the second, by vocation to the third. The relationship which binds all these together is more significant, more enduring than that of family, nation, or race. The dead, the living, and the yet unborn have God as their Father, Christ as their Brother, Mary as their Mother. There is among them a community of the most precious possession—love.

There is a give and take of assistance between those in purgatory and those in this life; and the saints in Heaven intercede for us. Here then is a doctrine which is at once a sublime ideal and a practical invitation to perpetual remembrance by the living of those who have gone before. Much more than a dream or a speculation, the communion of saints is something to be taken into our calculations when we struggle with temptation, or recite our morning prayers, or give an alms. Anyone of these things we can offer in behalf of those who have passed into the life beyond. It is a marked characteristic of our religion that the souls who have gone before are well remembered.

Dear Lord, I see in this doctrine a new reason for gratitude. I participate in the fellowship which brings together the ancient and the contemporary world. I can borrow strength from the knowledge of what has been achieved by saints far removed in time and space. I can offer help to souls who need it in the life beyond the grave. I will, with Your aid, be zealous both to increase the number of Your followers and also to bring no blot upon the reputation of the family which includes all who ever have borne, or ever will bear, Your name!

24th (and Last) WEEK AFTER PENTECOST—
SATURDAY

They Shall Never Perish (John 10, 28)

EXPECTATION of victory reinforces the will to win. The fact that hope greatly raises one's chances of success is stressed and underlined today, as it it were a modern discovery. Traditional Christian teaching, however, has always held that, in the supernatural as in the natural order, a well founded expectation of success is an indispensable element in effective striving. St. Paul says we are saved by hope; theology teaches that God always provides the help required to gain Heaven. The virtue of hope is classified with faith and charity; and these three theological virtues come together and increase together in the soul. There is no insuperable obstacle to the progress of the man who does his best.

On one condition, then, that we love God, "all things work together for good." But we must not overlook the condition, "that we love God." This means that we must be ready to contribute our best effort. Sufficient grace to succeed we may count upon; only a refusal to co-operate with grace can effectively block the road to Heaven. But our confidence is to be built on the twin supports of grace and good will; and only he that perseveres to the end will be saved.

Dear Lord, it is wholly beyond my power to put into words my sense of gratitude for this promise that You have given me. I could not possibly ask for more. Once again I affirm my love, my honor, my adoration. I look up to You in my lowliness, in the spirit which befits a creature raising His eyes to his Creator and Redeemer. You have promised that if I give myself to You. I shall be lifted up into that eternal life which is Yours; and I do give myself to You, now and forever, wholeheartedly, unreservedly, in faith, in hope, in love!